Th
La
Word

The Last Word

Insights About the Church and Ministry

WILLIAM H. WILLIMON

ABINGDON PRESS
NASHVILLE

THE LAST WORD
INSIGHTS ABOUT THE CHURCH AND MINISTRY

Copyright © 2000 by Abingdon Press

This book is printed on recycled, acid-free paper.

Library of Congress Cataloging-in-Publication Data

Willimon, William H.
  The last word : insights about the church and ministry / William H. Willimon.
    p. cm.
  ISBN 0-687-09002-4 (alk. paper)
  1. Church work—Meditations. 2. Clergy—Office—Meditations. I. Title.
  BV683.W55   2000
  253—dc21

                                                                00-044168

The "Last Word" columns were first published by The Christian Century Foundation in its *The Christian Ministry Magazine*. Used by permission.

Scripture quotations, unless otherwise noted, are taken from the New Revised Standard Version of the Bible. Copyright © 1989 by the Division of Christian Education of the National Council of the Churches of Christ in the United States of America. Used by permission.

Those noted RSV are from the *Revised Standard Version of the Bible,* copyright 1946, 1952, 1971 by the Division of Christian Education of the National Council of the Churches of Christ in the United States of America. Used by permission.

00 01 02 03 04 05 06 07 08 09—10 9 8 7 6 5 4 3 2 1

MANUFACTURED IN THE UNITED STATES OF AMERICA

To
my students at
Duke Divinity School

Contents

FOREWORD *Barbara Brown Taylor* 11

A FIRST WORD 15

1. PREACHING

A Tough Way to Make a Living 17
Feedback 20
What I'm Trying to Say Is 21
Sermon Slips 23
Sowing Rather Than Reaping 25
Sermons with Some Size 26
Poetic Preachers 28
The Rewards of Good Preaching 29
For God's Sake 32
Did You Hear What I Heard? 33
I'm Not OK, OK? 36
So You Want to Preach? 40
Talk About It 42
Talking About God 43
Sermon Outline 47

2. PEOPLE WHO ARE PASTORS

The Perils of *Not* Passing By on the Other Side 49
Pastoral Pugilism 52

The Extravagant Vocation 55
Practical Theology 57
Be Imitators of Me 59
Busy Pastors 60
I Was Vanna's Pastor 62
Just Say No 63
Influence Incognito 65
To Tell the Truth 67

3. WORSHIP

Give of Your Best to the Master 73
Meaning the Music 75
Fearful, Wonderful Worship 78
Quitting Time? 80
Great Moments in Worship 82
Getting Our Rites Right 83

4. CONGREGATIONAL LIFE

The Church Is Not Our Cadillac 85
Divine Wisdom Among Little Old Ladies 87
Ambiguous Epiphany 89
Be Reconciled 91
A Child's Sermon 93
Pat and Me 95
Keeping Work in Its Place 97
Ministry to Those *Not* in Crisis 99
The Visit 101
Pastoral Conversation 103
Ministrations 105
Do You Know Where Your Children Are? 108
The Reverend Grandma 110

5. EVANGELISM

Going Public with the Peculiar 113
Reaching Out to the Gloom and Doomers 115
Campus Ministry *In Loco Parentis* 117

Church Growth 119
Baby Boomer Bloopers 122
Operators Are Standing By 124
Secularity Lite 126
Open the Door 128
A Big Church 130
The Body of Christ 133
The Unassimilatable Mr. Gomes 134

Foreword

IN EVERY PROFESSION THERE ARE THINGS YOU DO not talk about. If you are a chef, you do not mention the weevils you picked out of the paprika before sprinkling it on your lobster thermidor. If you are a physician, you do not broadcast the fact that it is sometimes easier for you to recognize your patients by their body parts than by the names on their charts. If you are preacher, you do not publish your fantasy about slugging a parishioner in the jaw.

Unless you are Will Willimon, that is. Willimon talks about all kinds of things preachers are not supposed to talk about, such as nauseating children's sermons, martyrs on the altar guild, and the unabashedly pagan nature of most church weddings. Since he is as hard on himself as he is on everyone else, no one can accuse him of self-righteousness. His portraits of church life are so accurate that most readers will accuse themselves instead, if they can stop laughing long enough.

The genius of Willimon's humor is its power to disarm. He administers it the same way a dentist dispenses nitrous oxide, in order to get down to the business of healing, which begins by poking where it hurts. Once he has said all the unsayable things about irritating parishioners, clergy colleagues, and church hierarchies, he goes to work on the clergy themselves.

Laying his drill against some of the most sensitive nerves in

Christian ministry, he raises questions that linger long after the gas has worn off. When did we decide to preach sermons people could digest without chewing instead of offering them the same tough, gristly pieces of the gospel that keep us awake at night? When was the last time we conceived of a worship service as something designed to please God instead of to attract newcomers? At what point did we decide that justification by busyness was an acceptable alternative to justification by faith?

Readers of Willimon's other works will recognize familiar themes, as well as familiar tones of voice. In one essay, he praises an old seminary professor for teaching a class on Kierkegaard that was "abrasive, passionate, cynical, ironic." Willimon might as well have been speaking of himself. The only missing word is "truthful," which is the central virtue of these pieces. In a decade when popular novels about a cuddly clergyman named Father Tim have topped bestseller lists, it is vital to have an antidote on hand. Willimon's astringent prose promises to do the trick.

In snapshot after snapshot, he captures church people doing what we do best: maintaining appearances, defanging the gospel, and placating one another by alternating half-truths with outright lies. But some of his pictures also show another spirit at work. You can almost see it sometimes—a bright flash of light at the edge of the frame—as he focuses on the woman who drives an hour to church every Sunday so she can hear sermons that soar right over her head. You can see it in the members of the Alice Davis Memorial Circle of The United Methodist Women, who write letters of apology to the people of Vietnam and send portions of their Social Security checks to a refugee resettlement program. You can see it in the Duke graduate, who enrages her father when she decides to go on a three-year mission trip to Haiti instead of proceeding to medical school as planned.

They are all here, and they are all us: the flawed, the faithful, the focused, the scattered, the ones who make the angels laugh, along with the ones who make them weep. While none of us is simply one or the other, Willimon is not content to assure us that God loves us the way we are. Instead, he preaches a gospel that some of us may remember hearing somewhere before. God's passion for us is too deep to leave us as we are. We are destined for new life, and God means for us to bring the whole world with us when we come.

Barbara Brown Taylor
Demorest, Georgia

A First Word

WHEN IT COMES TO WORDS, THAT'S ALL THE WORLD is, all the way down, just words. That's good because that's about all we preachers have in our pastoral bag of tricks. Just words.

For the past couple of decades, I have been writing a column for pastors in *The Christian Ministry,* a column called "The Last Word." From time to time, some have urged me to collect those words into a book. This is that book. Sadly, it was completed during the same year that *The Christian Ministry* died, latest victim of the demise of mainline liberal Protestantism.

Nearly thirty years ago, I was ordained into the Christian ministry. On most days, I still find it a great wonder that, out of all those who could have done it as well as or better than I, God called me. This book contains the ad hoc pastoral theology of someone who, despite the many blessings of ministry, had to keep coming up with reasons for keeping at ministry.

My colleague Barbara Brown Taylor, in her Foreword, notes the humor in these pastoral meditations. I don't know how I could have kept at the demands of ministry if it were not for the humor. When I hear the word *grace*, I think of those moments in ministry when God gives us the ability to laugh at, rather than to cry over, the church. I hope my many smiles at the gap between who I am and who I ought to be, the gap between who the church is and who it is called to be, will not offend. However, if I herein offend, remember that I'm a preacher who is paid to preach the gospel on a weekly basis, so offense and wounded sensibilities come with the territory.

There are more than fifty-two meditations in this book, enough to read one for every week of a pastor's year, if you would like to read them that way. Or there are enough to read every day during the fall stewardship campaign, or one for every weekday during the summer doldrums if these words will help you to survive. In short, there ought to be enough of these for a pastor to use in order to muster the courage to keep at ministry during even the most trying times.

I hope that you will find comfort in these words, comfort that engenders constancy in ministry. If my words on ministry can help you to keep saying a good word for Jesus for the rest of your ministry, then I will not have written in vain, and these words will be, despite my many limitations, God's grace for you and the church.

William H. Willimon
June 17, 2000
Twenty-eighth anniversary of my ordination

Section 1 | Preaching

A Tough Way to Make a Living

I HATE WORDS.

See? That's not the best way to begin, but it was all I could come up with. Miss McDaniel taught me always to begin with a topical sentence "which encapsulates, in no more than ten words, everything you are trying to say in the essay." But in her sixth-grade class we were always writing about easy subjects like "The Future of My Country." Here it's different. Try to say something on a really important subject, and all of the right words duck for cover. So all I can think of to say is, I hate words.

That's the thing about words. You can't buy the right one when you need it. When you don't need words—say, when you're supposed to be quietly, empathetically listening to a parishioner—your words ooze out over everything, nervously filling all the empty spaces. You can't stop talking. But Saturday night, after a tough week—pulpit waiting for you like a hangman's rope in a few hours, you staring at a blank sheet of paper—where are all those words?

Words are as common as dirt on television or during a presidential campaign, but before a couple of parents whose four-year-old has just died of cancer, you can't get a good word for love or money.

Augustine referred to himself derisively as a "word merchant." That's us on Sundays. All we've got to offer, the only thing standing between us and God, is these words. There are gods who get close to people through war, or sex, or nature. Unfortunately for us preachers, our God, the God of Israel and the church, loves words. If we want to get to this God, it's through words or not at all. God speaks and the world springs into being (*ex nihilo*). I can't even get a coherent sentence when I need it on Sunday. It's a tough way to make a living.

As for me, I like to be in control. I don't expect to be brilliant, just to know where all of this is going to end by noon. Yet these words keep slipping from my grasp, jumping the tracks, getting lost in the congregation, whooping it up, running naked down the aisles.

I tell myself, "After all, this is *my* sermon." Then, scarcely have the words left my mouth (you can see it on people's faces as they sit and listen) my words have been adopted, purloined as *their* words. They're not even waiting for the sermon to be over. Already they are working on sermons of their own, taking over words that were first mine. You can't keep words in their place.

So they say, at the front door of the church after the sermon, "That really was a great sermon about . . . "

And I listen, but I can't hear my sermon. It's no good to say, "You idiot! My sermon was not about that; it was about this."

Too late. The words are now running loose, frolicking about the congregation, stirring up all manner of mischief, dressing up in different clothes. Someday these let-loose words will come back to haunt you, make you wish you had never gone out in public with that word.

I put my words down on sheets of paper. "There, that ought to hold you," I think to myself. Even there, in print, they will not stay in place. Paper and print give the illusion of stability and permanence. I just threw away the dictionary that got me through college, because so many of the words had changed definitions. And I'm not all that old.

No wonder someone is always misunderstanding, misconstruing my words. I say, "Well, what I meant to say was. . . ." But it's no good. The words are gone, set loose. I asked an old preacher what had he learned in his fifty years in the pulpit and he replied, "The possibilities for being misunderstood are infinite."

A few years ago, I did a book on burnout among the clergy. I was surprised (why should I have been?) to hear, in my interviews with clergy, that one of the most debilitating, depressing aspects of pastoral work was preaching. Blame it on the words.

I learned how great a challenge it is to give yourself, week after week, to so fragile an art. We work, chiseling these sermons out of the hard granite of the biblical text. We speak. Our words bounce off the walls, ricochet off the ceiling, and then die, soaked up by the pew cushions, or else burrowed deep in people's brains, waiting for the proper time to hatch, to jump you from behind as they say, "A few weeks ago, didn't you say in a sermon. . . ?"

I hate words. They're always changing hats, putting on airs, taking up residence at another address, mocking you, saying, "I don't mean that. I haven't meant that since late in the Bush administration. Now I mean . . ."

Words like *gay* or *girl* or *preacher* are too nimble on their feet. The other day, in a meeting, someone said that we needed to "*massage* this plan a little longer before it's ready."

Who invited a word like that into a meeting like this?

Some words grow limp with use, overuse. Once we could truly celebrate something. Then the church got hold of the word, preachers started celebrating this, celebrating that. When everything was a celebration, nothing was left to celebrate. Just the other day I saw *liberation, freedom,* and *community*—all words with a distinguished past—on their way out to the lexical cemetery. Now I'm forced to search for substitutes. Many perfectly good words refuse to work for clergy, probably because they've heard of how we've abused their relatives.

Otherwise respectable words like *commitment, stewardship, witness,* and *evangelistic* have now been transmogrified into a sort of sweet ooze. Use them on Sunday and watch the congregation's eyes glaze over. I hate the way words do that.

It's only four days until I've got to come up with something to say on Sunday. This is not a promising beginning. I'm groping. My mind has degenerated into an article from *Reader's Digest*. I have become a linguistic loser on *Wheel of Fortune*. Somebody get me Roget on the phone. I'm not even sure if I know what the word *means* means. If I can't get six or eight good words to end this "Last Word," what hope is there for the Sunday sermon? They're hiding. They wouldn't be seen dead in this article. I'm sounding ridiculous. My readers' eyes are glazing over. A word, a word, my kingdom for one lousy word. Miss McDaniel is ashamed of me. I hate words.

Unfortunately, the only cure for this or any other human malady is more words.

Feedback

In my seminary homiletics class, I invited a panel of local pastors to discuss with the students the subject of preaching. One student asked the panel, "How do you feel when people criticize your sermons?"

To the student's surprise, none of the pastors seemed to resent criticism of his or her preaching. "Preaching really begins when someone says, 'I didn't like what you said about so-and-so,'" explained one pastor. As far as preachers are concerned, *any* feedback, even negative, is better than none.

I suppose I feel that way as a writer. Or do I? The other day I was going through the thick file that I labeled "Response to Writing." If feedback is nourishment for a preacher, then I am well fed. For instance, after "a practical magazine for thinking clergy" published my marvelously candid revelation about my pastoral relationship with Vanna White, someone wrote to the editor:

"To whom it may concern:

"I just read your magazine. In particular, the article in the Last Word section. Question: IS THIS A JOKE? Is this star-stunned ding-dong really a pastor? Is this actually an 'impractical magazine for unthinking clergy'?"

Following a soul-searching piece on canine evangelism, a bishop wrote to me, "Unfortunately, the *United Methodist Book of Discipline* does not allow me to touch you, but if I were your bishop, I would have you in hot water before you could say 'boo.'"

Or perhaps before I could say "bark"?

On another occasion, someone who identified herself as having "given a lifetime to peace and justice ministry" told me, "Your article made me so mad I think that you ought to be shot. You have done great damage to the cause of peace in our church by your terrible ideas."

Pistol-packing pacifists.

Criticism of liberal theology won me this fusillade: "No, Dr. Willimon, we will not march back into the dark ages of narrow-mindedness, bigotry, and closed thinking. If I had my way, you would be banished from the pages of every church magazine, defrocked and silenced."

Just imagine what he would do to me if he weren't open-minded.

In response to a book I wrote on denominational decline, someone said, "I agree that you are right on many of your points and, to a great extent, you are right. But I do not support your right to say these things in a book published by your own denomination."

Sometimes one doesn't have the right to write what is right. Even if one is not on the right it doesn't pay to be in the right.

Please keep those cards and letters coming. Preachers like me love to know that they are being heard.

On second thought, just keep those cards and letters.

What I'm Trying to Say Is . . .

My colleague Richard Lischer plans to give the students in his introductory preaching classes a list of stories and illustrations that have collapsed into clichés because preachers have used them too often. That's the trouble with us preachers. When we find a good story or perfect illustration, we steal it back and forth from one another and use and reuse it until it goes limp.

Once, we had three successive guest preachers in the Duke University Chapel end their sermons with the story of the boy on the gallows from Elie Wiesel's novel *Night*. It's a moving, evocative, and powerful story, but it had lost its punch by the third telling. If we preachers can enervate so powerful a story, how much less effective do we make our weaker illustrations?

A myriad of once-good stories need to die a dignified death. Among them are

- He ain't heavy, he's my brother
- Christ has no hands but our hands
- Frederick Buechner's vision of a departed friend
- Will Campbell's "Easter Chicken"
- Reynolds Price's baptism dream story

Use any of these and watch the congregation's eyes glaze over.

Then there's the problem of stock words and phrases. We tend to dip into this storehouse when things aren't going well in the sermon, when we are groping for what to say next or buying time until we can remember our second point:

- Today I'd like you to consider . . .
- Some of you are saying to yourselves that this text is (fill in the blank: irrelevant; weird; not in the Bible; not worth a sermon), but I say to you that (in twenty minutes I can show you why it's important; it's in the lectionary, so who are you to say?; Jesus didn't really mean this the way it sounds) . . .
- Moving right along . . .
- Back to today's assigned text . . .
- One time there was a (little boy; little girl; squirrel) . . .
- Many of you are saying to yourselves . . .
- In conclusion . . .
- Finally . . .
- One last, quick comment . . .
- If time permitted . . .
- Maybe next Sunday I'll be able to explain . . .
- Well, you see what I'm driving at is . . .
- Finally, let us pray . . .
- It's perhaps best summed up in the words of (the old hymn; the poem by Robert Frost; that witty saying by Winston Churchill) . . .
- Again, let me reiterate . . .

We preachers not only bring our people close to God, we also protect them from God—often without knowing that we're doing so. One way we keep them safe from divine incursion is by talking about holy things in a way that devalues them. Therefore, one essential homiletical discipline is custody of the tongue, vigilance against the creeping cliché. Talk about God ought not to be cheap.

Sermon Slips

A deep, irrational fear grips every preacher—the fear of inadvertently saying something inappropriate, tasteless, suggestive, or just plain stupid while preaching. Preachers have been known to wake up screaming in the middle of the night, haunted by nightmares of saying something that doesn't come out the way they intend, in front of five hundred people. A slip of the tongue in the middle of a sermon is called "Freudian" by some, "evidence of the humility-producing power of the Holy Spirit" by others.

There is no way to get out of a sermonic slip, no matter how hard you try. You can't go back and explain. It is best to have the congregation immediately stand for the benediction.

I was preaching in a large auditorium in the West. Jet lag had taken its toll—at least that's the best excuse I can find. The person who introduced me had told the crowd of students that I was a great preacher, much in demand, interesting, controversial, and expensive. The pressure was on.

I launched into my sermon, a simple piece unworthy of such an extravagant introduction. "When the sermon is weak, say it louder," somebody once told me. So I was loud, emotional, passionate.

"And what is the most significant event our faith has to offer?" I asked. "The erection!" I bellowed.

Someone in the front row screamed.

"I mean the *resurrection!*" I said the correct word at least twelve more times. It didn't seem to do any good. Church was out.

"I'm sure I shall remember your sermon for the rest of my life," a young woman told me after the service. I could hear her laughing as she walked out of the building and down the street.

On another occasion, I was speaking in the Midwest. I spoke mightily, and at length, perhaps being too attentive to how I was speaking rather than to what I was saying. Afterward, as we left the auditorium, I hesitantly asked my host—who could be intimidating at times—"Well, how do you think it went?"

"Rather well," he said. I sighed in relief. "Except for a couple of small matters," he continued. "Jesus was born in Bethlehem, not Jerusalem. Matthew was a tax collector, not a Pharisee. And the capital of Iowa is Des Moines, not Cedar Rapids."

Picky, picky, picky.

A distinguished yet insufferably pompous evangelist was preaching before a gathering of Presbyterian ministers. He was attacking moral decadence, particularly sexual sin in contemporary society—risky business for a preacher prone to sermonic slips.

"I remember," he shouted, "when we looked up to women, expected them to set the moral tone for society. We placed them on a pedestal of honor. But not anymore. Have you seen the scandalous way women dress today?"

To illustrate his dubious point, he offered his former organist as an example. "Our organist, a precious young woman, came to practice for the service, dressed in a pair of short, tight, hiked-up running shorts. It was disgraceful! Walking into the Lord's house in those skimpy tight shorts. I determined to do something about it. It was my duty as a pastor. I confronted her and asked her to come down to my study and talk about it. I shared Scripture with her and told her how those shorts looked. And I'll tell you, in fifteen minutes I had those shorts off of her!"

He tried desperately to win back the hysterically laughing congregation, but he tried in vain. Each time he attempted to go on with his sermon, some corner of the congregation would erupt into renewed laughter.

So he asked them to stand for the benediction.

Sowing Rather Than Reaping

On Sunday morning, after I'm through preaching at Duke Chapel and have retired to my appointed perch, the seat behind the second sopranos where I blend into the woodwork, I often look up at the stained-glass window high above and across from me that depicts Moses. Only the second sopranos and I can see it. The window depicts scenes from Moses' life: the child raised by royalty, the angry defender of the oppressed, the liberator, the lawgiver, the leader of Israel to the promised land.

But often—at about 11:45—the sun highlights one scene more than the rest. It's the last event in Moses' ministry, when God prevents him from entering Canaan. Yahweh lets Moses get to the door but does not allow him to cross the threshold with Israel. Whether the artist who created these windows intended to force the preacher to ponder that scene week in and week out, I do not know. But I have memorized it in detail. As I look at the end of Moses' ministry, I am reminded of my own ministry.

A lot goes unfinished in it. Much of pastoral life is spent on the verge, at the door. Preaching takes the congregation to the threshold, but what good does it do?

As I recently worked on a book concerning ministerial burnout, on why pastors call it quits, I was impressed that preaching—a central pastoral activity—is a major source of pastoral disillusionment. It's such a fragile art. Much of the time that it takes to prepare a sermon is invisible—and so are the results. No one can demonstrate empirically verified results of "good" preaching. And that's a problem in a world that worships results.

For me and for the sopranos, we must, like Moses, be content with planting, and leave the harvest for others. They sing, I preach, and God only knows where it all leads, what land of promise will be opened through our ministry.

A man I know who works with teachers says the ones who are best able to keep at it over the years are those "who are good sowers rather than good reapers." Teachers and preachers must find meaning enough in the act of planting the seed and not in the need to be there for the harvest.

If we preachers or choir members or Sunday school teachers are going to persevere at Christian ministry we will do so only by having confidence that God really does convey treasure through us earthen vessels. God really does put us to good purposes. Even though we may not understand God's plans, even though we may not enter the promised land of concrete results and visible fulfillment, we can boldly announce the message of the ultimate triumph of God's good purposes to those in exodus, going from here to there.

Sermons with Some Size

I have just finished preaching a sermon that elicited the comment, "That little sermon was so wonderfully simple, anyone could have understood your point."

It was meant as a compliment. Somehow it didn't sound like one. I remembered a passage in Richard Baxter's "The Reformed Pastor" (in Thomas Wood, ed., *Five Pastorals* [London: SPCK, 1961], pp. 209-37), which, with only an afternoon of searching, I found. After noting that "it is most desirable that the minister should be of parts above the people so far as to be able to teach them, and awe them," Baxter advises preachers to sometimes preach sermons that are intentionally so large as to "stall the understandings" of the congregation:

"See that you preach to such auditors as these some higher points that stall their understandings, and feed them not with all milk but sometimes with stronger meat; for it exceedingly puffs them up with pride when they hear nothing from ministers but that they know already or can say themselves. . . . Not that I would have you neglect the great fundamental verities, or wrong the weak and ignorant people while you are dealing with such as these; but only when the main part of your sermons is as plain as you can speak, let some one small part be such as shall puzzle these self-conceited men; or else have one sermon in four or five on purpose for them . . . and let them see that it is not your obscure manner of handling but the matter itself that is too hard for them, and so may see that they are yet but children that have need of milk, and that you would be more upon such higher points if it were not that their incapacity doth take you off" (p. 233).

When is the last time I preached in such a way as to stall the understandings of my auditors? The day of the "pulpit prince" (or princess) appears to be over. Few congregations will sit still for a forty-five-minute theological address. And yet ought we contemporary preachers to be embarrassed that nothing in our sermons stalls the understanding? Too many of us are adept in pulpit communication that demands little of our hearers, the gospel reduced to a bumper sticker slogan or three easy points that are so easy to remember as to be not worth remembering.

So I think Baxter would agree with Walter Brueggemann when he says of contemporary preaching, "Where the sense of largeness is lacking, . . . sermons are twittered away in good advice, happy reassurances, or harsh intimidation" ("Some Missing Prerequisites," *Journal of Preachers* [Fall 1989], p. 27).

I remember my old teacher of preaching saying that his aunt always insisted on going with him to hear Paul Tillich preach whenever he preached at Yale. She came away having understood absolutely nothing from Tillich's Teutonic accent or abstractions, but utterly thrilled at having understood that she was present where something very significant had been said. A person could spend a Sunday morning in less edifying ways.

Then there was the person whom I met at a wonderful little Anglo-Catholic parish outside of Boston. At the church's coffee hour, I asked her why she commuted one hour each way to this little church. She explained to me that a friend had brought her here for one of the priest's lectures on "Great Doctrines of the Church."

"He lectured nonstop for forty-five minutes," she said. "Something about the trouble at Nicea. It was wonderful!"

"What was so wonderful about it?" I wanted to know.

"I didn't understand any of it!" she replied. "It was utterly, wonderfully incomprehensible. And I am a Vassar graduate! I've never missed a Sunday since then."

I surmise that she was so fatigued with short little sermons, on superficial little subjects, well-illustrated chats which belabor the obvious, that she was thrilled to come up against something that was bigger than she, Vassar grad though she was.

If our preaching would form congregations adequate to the challenge of discipleship in today's world, we need some sermons with some size.

Poetic Preachers

A professorial friend of mine defines hell as being "trapped in an elevator with people who believe *the* is a verb." I would counter with a definition of heaven: It is the place where everyone talks like H. Louis Patrick.

Patrick, longtime pastor of Charlotte, North Carolina's Trinity Presbyterian Church and past preacher on "The Protestant Hour," can preach for me anytime. He uses a muscular English that is poetic without being contrived or showy. Every single word is correctly placed. Surely God is pleased by such preaching. Patrick is said to be a sort of godfather to another artist-preacher, Frederick Buechner, who dedicated one of his recent books to Patrick. It takes an artist to know one.

I once thought Patrick's sermons should stick a bit closer to the biblical text. I wanted him to demonstrate more of his hermeneutics, to show us how he moved from text to sermon. But what did I know? My dry, dull, from-point-A-to-point-B exegesis would be too prosaic, too pedestrian for Patrick. If something can't be said with some grace, with some gentle twist of the tongue, why say it? His sermons are Matthew, Mark, and Luke filtered through Frost, Sandburg, and C. S. Lewis. He sounds like God, if God were fortunate enough to have a good bass voice and to have been from Due West, South Carolina.

I used to put down those pulpit princes of the past, those pastors who did nothing but preach, specializing in giving their congregations what Kierkegaard scornfully called "Sunday glimpses into eternity." But lately I've decided that a preacher could do worse than be a poet. I've heard—and preached—too many

"Saturday Night Specials," sermons that are a warmed-over goulash of trite clichés and inconsequential ideas, sermons better sucked through a straw than chewed on all week—Give me Patrick's poetry any day. Give me Gardner Taylor saying the word *redemption* twenty different ways in twenty minutes. Give me some old pulpit prince who still venerates the spoken word and considers it no small honor to give a glimpse of eternity to the woefully earthbound creatures who gather on Sunday morning.

As long as there is one person left to tell the Story, and tell it well, to consider heaven and hell hung between a mere word and the exact word, then all of us have hope. There will be a word because someone has loved the Word and us enough to give his or her life to the art of preaching.

When as a young preacher in my first parish, so intent on being useful to the church, I first heard Patrick's voice over the radio. It was something I never got over. I prayed to God for a voice like that, words like those. Patrick's sermons convinced me that I had my work cut out for me if I was going to be someone people called Preacher. I realized it would probably take me the rest of my life to live up to the name.

Walter Brueggemann notes that Israel's prophets are best thought of not as carping social critics or designers of political schemes for human betterment, but as poets. Through every artful means at their disposal, especially words—words rushing down like a mighty stream—they sought to make people weep and dream. They sought to find a worthy audience for God's poetry.

A friend told me of a conversation he had with an aging Hopi woman in Arizona. "Tell me about your children," he said.

"Well, I have two sons," she replied. "One is an engineer. The other is a poet. The poet is a practical one."

The Rewards of Good Preaching

"Why are so few people in our denomination really good preachers?" the impudent layperson asked.

I replied, "Because there are too few rewards for good preaching. No one sees all the work a preacher puts into a sermon. Too many of our clergy get to "the top" not through evaluations of their preaching but rather because they are 'good soldiers,' good at working the ecclesiastical system rather than good at working the biblical text." At least that's what I think.

Of course "good preaching" is not essentially known by the manuscripts it produces or the awards that words win. *Christian* preaching is always judged best by its effects. The preached word must be embodied, performed by the faithful, or it is miserable failure and I'm supposed to go home sick.

There I was, stuck with a testy text like Matthew 19:16-26: Jesus and the rich young man. Great. I'm supposed to stand up on the middle of a modern, elitist, secular, power-hungry university (is there any other kind?) and speak about Jesus causing a bad case of depression in an otherwise successful, upwardly mobile young adult? Give me a break.

In my sermon, I attempted to steer close to the text. This is a call story, I said. Someone is being called to follow Jesus. There's no way to sidestep that the story ends in despair. The young man's countenance falls, and Jesus notes the impossibility of saving the rich. As far as I can recall, this is the only call story in this Gospel where Jesus directly invites someone to discipleship and the person refuses. And the reason for the refusal? Money.

As I said, it's a tough text in my context.

So I preached it, restraining my inclination to explain away the culminating despair, trying hard not to tie it all up with a bow. After all, Matthew just lets it hang there, so why shouldn't I?

The next morning, Monday, in the breakfast line in the university cafeteria, I encountered the chair of the department of religion. "Well what happened yesterday?" he asked.

"Yesterday?" I asked.

"The sermon! Just couldn't think of an ending, could we? Sort of got it all out on the table but didn't know what to make of it, right?"

"Er, uh, right."

"Well, don't worry," he said. "You're usually quite adequate. Can't be good on every Sunday, can we?"

I staggered with my tray of grapefruit and raisin bran toward my table, but not before being intercepted by the dean of the divinity school.

"Did I feel for you in the service!" he said. "After that dull anthem, well, what hope was there for your sermon? There was no way for you to salvage things after that! You've got to demand that those musicians give you some help."

"Er, uh, right."

I collapsed at the table, slumped over the raisin bran.

A young man, graduate student in forestry, came up to me.

"That sermon," he said.

"Look kid," I said, "I may have to take crap off of them but I certainly don't have to take it off of you. Don't start on me about that sermon."

He looked confused (not a particularly unusual look for someone in forestry, I find). Then he continued, "You know me—religious experience in college, gave my life to Christ. I thought Jesus was supposed to be nice! I know someone told me that. I just went home and cried."

"You *cried*?" I asked.

"Yep, just lay on my bed and cried. I asked Jesus, 'Well, what do you want? What the heck do you want? Want me to give away my bike? Would that satisfy you? How about the stereo? What do you want from me?' "

"See that balding older man over there?" I asked. "I wish you would go over and explain that sermon to him in words of one syllable. He didn't get it. But thank God, you got it."

I did not get an award for that sermon. I received no special remuneration for delivering it in a well-modulated voice. Yet you preachers will understand what I mean when I say I don't care. I've had my reward. The proof of a sermon, a *Christian* sermon, is in its performance.

Sitting there at 8:00 A.M. in the college cafeteria on a Monday, I got my reward.

WILLIAM H. WILLIMON

For God's Sake

The Reverend Parker fidgeted with his railway watch, periodically retrieving it from his vest pocket, scowling at it, and thrusting it back into his pocket. Mrs. Parker attempted to calm him with her hand, hoping thereby to suggest to Mr. Parker that such preoccupation with a pocket watch was rude, particularly during someone else's sermon. But to no avail.

Mr. Parker was miserable. As a Methodist district superintendent, he was forced to visit churches in his district and endure other preachers' sermons, an administrative duty he clearly detested. All that fiddling with his watch was testimonial to his misery during this interminable sermon.

As for me, I lay low, staring placidly at the flailing preacher. Seated next to the Parkers, seated between them and the young woman I was courting, I could ill afford to attract attention to myself. I did not want to appear either to approve or to disapprove of the sermon being set before us. I could be sitting beside my future in-laws, after all.

The preacher did seem to be having problems, suffering, as he was, from a terminal case of indecision.

"We need to be more committed to Christ," he ventured, then quickly qualifying himself with "but not to the point of fanaticism; that would be a mistake."

Mr. Parker checked his watch yet again, this time with visible anguish.

"We need to fulfill our vows to the church," continued the preacher, "but not, of course, to the detriment of our other important responsibilities. No one wants that."

And on and on, homiletical death by a thousand qualifications and reservations.

At last the hesitant sermon ended, or rolled over and just died. We stood for the final hymn and then trudged out, the Parker family and I, the visiting boyfriend, trooping behind Mr. Parker toward his Buick in the back parking lot. Upon reaching his car, Mr. Parker grasped the handle of the door, wheeled around toward me and shouted:

"Young man, if God should call you into the ministry [I was then considering a call to go to seminary], and if God gives you a place to preach, and if God gives you anything to say to the people, *for God's sake say it!*"

It's not a bad thing for any of us preachers to remember. Mainline Protestantism seems to be suffering from a failure of theological nerve. Our trumpets suffer from our uncertain sound. The bland leading the bland.

Courage to speak arises, in great part, from the conviction that God has given us something to say. I recall Leander Keck (one-time dean of Yale Divinity School), in a debate on the most effective sermon styles, saying, "When the messenger is gripped by a message, the messenger will find the means to speak it."

As preachers, we know the challenge, in a relativistic culture, of standing up and daring to say, "This news is good; this word is true."

On one occasion Walter Brueggemann said to us, "If you are a coward by nature, don't worry. We can still use you. You can get down behind the biblical text. You can peek out from behind the text saying, 'I don't know if I would say this, but I do think the text does.'"

Courage to speak requires clarity about our source of authority. If we only stand in the pulpit to "share ourselves" or to "tell my story," as some misguided recent homiletics have urged us, then the church shall end, not with a bang but in a simpering sigh after a thousand qualifications and reservations.

This Sunday, take Mr. Parker's advice. If God gives you a word for God's people, *for God's sake say it!*

Did You Hear What I Heard?

In that wonderfully irreverent Monty Python creation, *The Life of Brian,* the Jesus-figure Brian is busy giving a sermon on the mount, or at least a hill. He pronounces, "Blessed are the peacemakers."

A poor soul hears, "Blessed are the *cheesemakers*."

"What's so special about them?" he asks someone standing next to him.

"I'm sure he meant to include all those who work with milk products," reassures the other man.

It's tough to be in the communication business.

The Holy Spirit descends, and those who were previously voiceless speak (Acts 2). The church understands their speech as the outbreak of truth-telling prophesied by the prophet Amos. The crowd in the street hears only the drunken babble of those who have indulged in new wine even before lunch.

We hear the words of Christ as words unto life, whereas nine out of ten of those surveyed said "it thundered" (John 12:29).

One of the insights of postmodern philosophy is the conviction that words have a power of their own, that language has an infinitely suggestive, evanescent, evocative quality that the speaker does not control. Communication is a much more conflicted activity than we earlier supposed.

Philosopher Jacques Derrida reads Plato's *Phaedrus* and hears Socrates use the Greek word *pharmakon,* which means in Greek both "cure" and "poison" (*Dissemination,* trans. B. Johnson [Chicago: University of Chicago Press, 1981], pp. 95-96, 129-30). Socrates is talking about how writing was introduced into civilization as a cure for the inability of human memory. Even though Plato says nothing in this dialogue concerning the ambiguous nature of language, Derrida hears a play on the double meaning of *pharmakon*. Language is both a remedy for our human weakness (cure) and a cause of human tragedy (poison). Furthermore, Derrida hears an echo of other similar-sounding Greek words like *pharmakos* ("scapegoat") and *pharmakeus* ("magician") and expounds on how language functions in these ways too.

Derrida is rather shockingly unconcerned whether or not Plato had any of these associations in mind when he used the word *pharmakon* to talk about language. Derrida's concern is the way language keeps on working even after the author's supposed original meaning has been comprehended; the way listeners take what a speaker says and run with it, running down paths of their own devising, taking speech in directions quite out of control of the speaker. The alleged intentions of the speaker are only one aspect of what is "really going on" in speaking. Language has a large life of its own, involves itself (to quote a typically Derridian phrase) in an "autonomous overassemblage of meanings."

Thus Derrida describes speaking as the anguished yet exhilarating experience of losing control. Roland Barthes speaks of how the word "shines with an infinite freedom," and plugs into an infinite number of "meanings, reflexes, and recollections" in the hearer (*Writing Degree Zero,* trans. A. Lavers and C. Smith [Boston: Beacon Press, 1970], p. 47). Derrida prefers to think of language not primarily as speech, but rather primarily as written symbols in order to stress the independent quality of language.

Those of us who are preachers, who are paid (though not paid well) to speak to, from, and for the church on a weekly basis, could also testify to the rather uncontainable, unmanageable quality of the spoken word.

At Pentecost, people hear, but they hear "everyone in his own language." Communication is far from uniform. There is more than one way to explain the intrusions of God. Revelation is always thick, multivalent, ambiguous—causing conflict in the street. What was it that was said? What am I supposed to do now?

And I hate to be out of control. I love to know where we will all be by noon on Sundays. I want to "deliver" a sermon like delivering a pizza. But no, between the workings of the Holy Spirit, to say nothing of our listeners' imaginations, things get muddled, expanded, taking thought in directions not of the preacher's devising.

Many times you have stood at the door of the church, after preaching your heart out, and had someone emerge from the service saying, "Preacher, that was a great sermon. I really agree with you when you said. . . ." And then the preacher hears the parishioner say something totally different from what the preacher *thought* was said in the sermon.

You want to say, "Wait a minute. I didn't say that."

But why waste your breath? Communication is a two-way affair; no, in the church, with the Spirit roaming and all, it's at least a *three*-way affair. What you actually said or meant to say is only one small part of the communication equation.

And I hate to be out of control.

A friend of mine who is a preacher, accompanied his wife, who is a lawyer, through a series of mock trials in which the law firm had hired a mock jury to listen to the lawyers argue in preparation for an upcoming case. Then, through closed-circuit TV, the lawyers watched the jurors process and vote on the case.

My friend the preacher, after watching the jurors discuss what they had heard in the trial, came away from the experience muttering to himself, "The ability of people to confuse communication is limitless."

True. But the ability of people, under the promptings of the Holy Spirit, to expand, reapply, be convicted by, have their lives permanently rearranged by communication is also, thank God, limitless. To preachers' surprise, and sometimes chagrin, the Spirit keeps on opening up meaning in our words, meaning we might not have dared intended.

You preach a sermon, just a little sermon with a few polite suggestions on how we ought to be more dedicated to Christian discipleship. At the end of the service, Joe Jones emerges from the church, tears in his eyes, saying, "Preacher, thank you. God spoke to me today. I'm selling my plumbing business and moving to Honduras to work with the poor in the name of Jesus."

And you are petrified. Someone has taken your little words, words not meant for such revolutionary purpose, and run with them.

And I hate to be out of control.

I'm Not OK, OK?

"A man was going down from Jerusalem to Jericho, OK? And on the way, OK? he fell among thieves who stripped him, OK? robbed him, OK? and left him half dead, OK? Now by chance there came down the road a priest, OK?. . ."

Sometime ago a friend of mine, an Episcopal priest, returned from a diocesan clergy retreat declaring that the "masters of social work degree may destroy the English language." He was particularly critical of those persons (many of whom, according to his reckoning, hold MSWs) who major in "process"—the ability to totally determine the direction of a group without anyone in the group knowing it.

Whether or not this disgruntled Anglican was correct in his condemnation of the linguistic leanings of those in the social sciences, I am confident that he would agree with my deep grammatical, maybe even spiritual, concern about the onslaught of *OK*.

When did this virus, the nefarious *OK*, first infect the English language? I don't know where the creeping *OK* originated, but I do know that it threatens to undermine an important function of speech, namely to express disagreement, displeasure, or disapproval of other people and what they say.

Under the guise of politeness, a speaker will pepper his or her conversation with random *OK*s in an unctuous attempt to imply that what he or she is saying to you is, well, *OK*.

"Today I want to talk to you, OK? for two hours on a subject of absolutely no interest to you, OK? And . . ." You get the picture. This is the ecclesiastical equivalent to the "I'm going to stick this dagger in your heart, OK? And you are going to act as if you love it, OK?"

From here these *OK*s multiply like rabbits. "Now folks, I'm just going to read the entire book of Leviticus, OK? And . . ."

I suppose that these gratuitous *OK*s are meant to mean something akin to "Do you understand what I am saying to you?" or "Am I saying this simply enough for you to figure out, Stupid?" *OK* thus assumes the position previously occupied by the now archaic, "Y'know?" and the nearly extinct "Am I lying or what?"

Perhaps it is meant to give the illusion that we are actually communicating, that I am in agreement with what you are saying to me, that I am delighted to be sitting here in this circle of metal chairs in the church fellowship hall spending a morning with you, that I have given you permission to speak. I have done nothing of the kind. You must earn your way into my brain without presuming that I am on your side, grammatically speaking. What am I supposed to say to the speaker's repeated *OK*? I have the impression that if I were to summon the courage to say, "No, it's not OK," the speaker would be deeply hurt, perhaps even turn violent. My experience with these nondirective types suggests that they are most dangerous when cornered. Their smile, while repeatedly saying "OK," is positively psychotic. An unctuous smile, mixed with a heavy dose of *OK*, when present in someone with an MSW degree, is like nitrogen laced with glycerin.

Take my word for it. Communicative imperialism lurks behind the apparently innocent *OK*. Through the *OK*, the speaker claims consensus, implies that we're all together on this, insinuates a level of group cohesion, and suggests that we may eventually get married.

"OK, let's start the meeting, OK? And here's what we're going to do, OK? I'll tell you what we need to do today and you listen, OK? Then you'll vote as I tell you, OK?"

And it's not just done in groups at meetings.

A large nurse greets me at the door of the psychiatric unit, smiling at me menacingly, addressing me in the same tone of voice that is used when talking to a class of kindergartners, the same tone that people like her assume just before they stick patients with long needles. "I'm on the staff here in this ward of the hospital, OK?"

I ask myself, "How should I know if that's OK? We've just met. Show me your résumé and a copy of your college transcript, and I'll give you an opinion on whether or not you should be employed here."

Wedging her body squarely between me and the door, one foot planted firmly behind the door just in case I try to storm the ward and make an unauthorized pastoral visit, she continues, "And in the interest of patient care, OK?, not just our own attitudes toward clergy, OK?, the staff has found it good to limit clergy visitation to twenty minutes a morning, OK?"

See? When you hear *OK*, *en garde*. It's a signal, a tip that you are about to get shafted, verbally speaking.

"And since it's already eleven, you'll need to return tomorrow, OK?" Here it becomes clear that the *OK* is being used like the grape jelly my mother used to coat an aspirin in order to get me to swallow it, or the chocolate coating of some foul-tasting laxatives.

Her *OK?* suggests that you enjoy being turned away from her door, that you've had some sort of discussion about it, that it's all OK.

Her final *OK?* does the deal. For me to respond with, "But I've driven two hours to get here and I can't come back tomorrow," after being stroked, massaged, and fondled by this insidious barrage of *OK*s would be to appear incredibly disagreeable. Now, after all of these good-humored, solicitous *OK*s, there is nothing left for me to say but "OK."

Grammar becomes algebra, in which a set consecutive "OK? ...OK? ...OK?" will always produce the sum of *OK*.

Of course, in ecclesiastical situations, the *OK* is certain to spread like North Carolina kudzu. There's no stopping it, because in church we are all forced to be nice no matter what—just the sort of fertile breeding ground where the *OK* flourishes. The *OK* enables manipulative, coercive, and otherwise difficult persons to appear to be loving, caring, communal, and nice.

"Pastor, the Administrative Board has asked me to talk with you, OK?"

Why shouldn't it be perfectly OK with me to be fired, sacked, given the old heave-ho in such cowardly fashion? I therefore say, "OK."

"And while we really respect the work you've been able to do here in your first year, OK?, and while we know that you have many responsibilities, you know that things have been tight around here this year, OK? . . ."

Ah, yes. Cutting my way with machete through the dense undergrowth of *OK*s, I see what we're coming to—money.

"So the Board wanted me to see if, OK? it would be OK for you not to have a raise this year. OK?"

To this wonderfully charitable proposal—and delivered with such compassion, too—I, now robbed of any shred of human dignity, of course responded, "I'm OK, and you're OK, and it's OK."

Standing on my front porch, 9:00 P.M.:

"Mr. Willimon, I'm Bryan, OK? I've come to pick up your daughter, OK? We're just going to mess around until midnight, OK?"

When I attempt to strangle the young man to death with my bare hands, my only defense is temporary syntactical insanity. OK?

So You Want to Preach?

Dear Dr. Willimon:

Someday I would like to preach like you. I like your style. Could you advise me on which preparation would be best?

(Name withheld by request)

So you want to preach?
Good.
Be birthed by a mother who, like old Hannah, uses you as a
    bargaining chip with God,
Promising to give you to God right after she's done with you.
Or be abandoned by your mother (or even better, father),
left as an orphan so frail you must run to God for keeping.
Either way will do.

So you want to preach?
Have a storm-tossed, tormented youth.
Burn with passion's fires, satiate your desires.
Or be the all-American boy,
President of the church youth group,
Eagle in your Boy Scout troop,
Model of morality for all teens less chaste to admire.
Later, some congregation will feed like a hog on all your pent-
    up, unused desire.

So you want to preach?
Fall in love with words.
Collect clichés and burn them.
Imitate every well-wrought voice you hear.
Like Francis, exhort the birds.
Read all the plays (sonnets too) of Shakespeare.
(Anyone who despised God that much, and so eloquently too,
    must be of interest to a would-be word peddler like you.)

So you want to preach?
Poach from the poems of Yeats, consume the short stories of
    O'Connor. Crib Augustine's *Confessions*. Swipe Schweit-
    zer's *Quest*.
Steal the opinions of others before attempting any of your own.
    This way, time honored, is best.
Oh, yes, the novels of Walker Percy, the entire Sunday *Times*.
But never, never bother with anthologies of religious rhymes.

So you want to preach?
Fall in love, and out again.
Be in pain.
Get lost. Roam.
Come back home.
Get saved.
In sin be bold.
Walk out past the street lights; sit alone long nights in the cold

So you want to preach?
Good. Nothing bad ever happened to a preacher; Wednesday's
    tragedy is fodder for Sunday's sermon.
A marital separation can be useful, or an unsuccessful opera-
    tion.
Stare at yourself naked in the mirror; stare at your people when
    doing visitation.
Listen to their lives, their lies, their dreams, their hopes.
Keep notes.
Listen.
The things in life that hammer, wrack, and confuse,
These, a homiletician knows how to use.

So you want to preach?
Attend one of our first-rate theology schools.
Read all the required texts; make friends with God's fools.
Increase your vocabulary of swollen words that end in "-tion."
Half of this will be worthless, dated, scarcely ten years into
    your ministry.
Yet what's not will preserve you from theological insanity.

Later, when your words fail, as they will, and your ministry
gives you reason for pause,
Remember, the God of Israel, the Bible tells us, has always
been a sucker for the lost cause.

Talk About It

David Augsburger, professor of pastoral care at Fuller, relates
the story of how once, a group of Mennonite pastors were meeting to discuss the issue of the church's response to sexual abuse.
In his remarks to the pastors, Augsburger noted that something
like 1 in 4 women are, at some time in their lives, victims of sexual abuse. Therefore, it is reasonable to assume that an average of
about 1 in 4 of our parishioners who are women might seek pastoral care for help in dealing with this problem. Yet, when asked,
only 1 pastor out of the 64 present had ever counseled a parishioner on this issue.

Augsburger asked, "How many of you have ever made explicit reference to this issue in a sermon?" Only one pastor in the
group had.

The group then made a covenant. In the next six months of their
sermons, they agreed to make at least ten statements about the
injustice of sexual abuse.

At the end of six months, the group met again. Out of the group
of pastors who gathered, virtually *all* had women in their congregations who had come to them seeking counseling as they strug-
gled with their victimization by sexual abuse.

One of the great functions of preaching is the naming of pain,
the bringing to speech of those matters we find too painful or too
mysterious to talk about. A word on some difficult matter in a
sermon often becomes an open door to further discussion within
the congregation—a gracious invitation by the pastor for communal discussion of those things that matter but that are often
swept under the congregational carpet. Preaching can be a prelude
to significant pastoral care. On the other hand, as Augsburger's
story illustrates, when such matters are never mentioned in ser-

mons, we pastors can be sending unconscious signals that some conversation is out of bounds within the congregation and that certain human pain is beyond the reach of divine healing.

A number of years ago, on my way to visit in the hospital, I heard a lengthy discussion on my car radio of the then upcoming Supreme Court decision on abortion. I realized that, though all of America was debating the issue of abortion, I had never mentioned this subject in a sermon. With great homiletical courage, I resolved to enter these treacherous waters. A few Sundays later, I spoke on my own wrestling with the issue of abortion, speaking as if I were courageously bringing this matter to the attention of my benighted congregation.

Well, you know what happened. The next week, no fewer than six different parishioners approached me for further conversation on the subject, six parishioners who had *already* been struggling with abortion in their lives or in the lives of their families. I had not been the first to arrive on the scene of this dilemma.

"My only regret is that you didn't preach that sermon a year ago," said one of them.

Few things are better left unsaid. Sometimes, in my great zeal for and practice of lectionary-based preaching, I leave too many important matters out of congregational conversation. While the Bible does not speak to every human concern and, while I see no reason for the church to make a public statement or to adopt an official position on every matter of public controversy, all of us preachers ought to do an inventory of all the important, troubling issues we have never brought to speech. There ought to be a greater congruence between our pastoral care struggles and our Sunday morning pulpit subjects.

Think about it. Talk about it.

Talking About God

Halford Luccock, that great teacher and preacher, told the story of the Methodist congregation in the remote Dakotas who suffered a severe blizzard one winter. The snow was high. Even the mail did not get through for a week, which meant the pastor and congregation had no clue what was the denominational emphasis for that week in February. They did not know if it was United Nations Sunday or the Festival of the Christian Home Sunday.

So, said Luccock, the pastor strode embarrassed before the congregation that Sunday and said, "In the absence of any other reason for gathering, we'll just worship God."

I was ordained in 1972. The day after, my denomination, which had known only growth, began to lose members. Although there is some evidence that our decline is leveling off, the past two decades will be remembered by mainline Protestants, almost without exception, as the time of The Great Decline.

Most of us began worrying about our membership losses with the publication of Dean Kelley's *Why Conservative Churches Are Growing* (Harper & Row, 1977). Kelley's thesis, as best I remember, was not that conservative churches were growing simply because they were strict and conservative (although their relatively high demands upon their members were a positive growth factor) but rather because these churches kept themselves energetically focused on the main business of religion—making meaning for their members. When churches become distracted, seeing themselves as just another volunteer service organization or one more friendly social club, they decline. The business of churches, said Kelley, is meaning in God.

In the succeeding years, we pastors were deluged by studies and books on church growth and decline. Some said Kelley had neglected certain sociological factors; that he had made too much of the intellectual/theological basis for church growth. They pointed out that the mainline Protestant birth rates had declined since the 1950s. Most mainline growth comes through births to members, therefore the decline.

Others noted that the decline, which was noticeable only by the end of the 1960s, had actually begun much, much earlier (see Roger Finke and Rodney Stark, *The Churching of America, 1776–1990* [Rutgers, 1992]). Others noted that the mainline was burdened by a high proportion of churches in older, decaying neighborhoods, which rendered them ill-suited for the challenges of a mobile population. David A. Roozen and Dean R. Hoge, in *Understanding Church Growth and Decline* (Pilgrim, 1979), emphasized that the denominational culture of mainline Protestant denominations mitigated against growth. We were good at maintaining the status quo but poor at mobilizing for mission.

Yet there was a sense in which Kelley's thesis continued to haunt some of us. Was a major factor in our decline something to do with meaning, that is, something to do with God? Had we unknowingly withdrawn from the main business of the church?

A recent book by C. Kirk Hadaway and David A. Roozen, *Rerouting the Protestant Mainstream: Sources of Growth and Opportunities for Change* (Abingdon, 1995), shows the fruit of decades of studies of church growth and decline. As their title shows, Hadaway and Roozen, two distinguished observers of the mainline church, want to get beyond analysis and more toward positive prescription.

We live in a buyer's market, as far as religion is concerned, say Hadaway and Roozen. And that's not completely bad. Having had a virtual monopoly on American religious life, today's mainline Protestants must now adapt to a consumerism culture where people shop for a church, demand quality, and drop their church if it doesn't meet their demands.

Too often those demands are identified as an upbeat worship service, a clean nursery, and a big parking lot—which are important factors. However, Hadaway and Roozen highlight a demand that echoes some of Kelley's earlier claims. They say that, when all the factors are studied, "the key issue for churches seems to be a compelling *religious* character..., not whether the content of that character is liberal or conservative" (p. 69). In other words, Kelley was right. It is not so much that conservative churches are conservative, it is that they stick to the business of providing a theological rationale for people's lives. They keep focusing on God.

I had said, "Mainline Protestantism is in trouble because we provided people with the theological rationale not to go to church. We gave them a theology of secularity." Hadaway and Roozen seem to agree. Church cannot be a sanctified form of Rotary. We must clearly, intentionally, relentlessly be determined to be a place where we meet God and God in Jesus Christ meets us.

Hadaway and Roozen tell the delightful story of a Roman Catholic congregation that opened its worship with a time of friendly community and hand-shaking. The priest said, "It would be a shame to leave here without knowing those around us."

Then, with a twinkle in his eye he said, "It would be a much greater shame to leave here without knowing God!"

The congregation erupted into applause as if to affirm *that* was *the* reason they were there.

Hadaway and Roozen are explicit: "To grow and to continue growing, it is necessary for each mainstream church to become a vital *religious* institution, vibrant with the presence of God. It must develop a clear *religious* identity, a compelling *religious* purpose, and a coherent sense of direction that arises from that purpose" (p. 86).

A strong sense of identity and a compelling vision are the two essential characteristics for a vibrant congregation. Hadaway and Roozen are critical of Kelley and others who believe that high demands, conservative theology, and strict expectations are the key.

We desperately need leaders, say Hadaway and Roozen, leaders who are unsatisfied with decline, who refuse to bow to sociological determinism, who emphasize the distinctive, spiritual, God-dimensions of church. Church growth is *not* the point. The point is vital witness, in word and deed, to the presence of God in our midst. We've got to get over our liberal dis-ease with the theological rationale for the church. Hadaway and Roozen accuse us of a "don't-ask-don't-tell" policy in regard to God. We replaced "the intensity of religious experience for a reasoned civility" (p. 127).

I bring all this up because you, as a preacher, have as your responsibility to tell us the story, to lay God upon us, to name the Name that is above every Name, to "offer Christ" (Wesley). Our great vocation is not to offer rules for better living, helpful hints for homemakers, guidelines for self-esteem. We are to help the church to talk about God.

I recall James Sanders, a great Hebrew Bible scholar, giving us a hermeneutical principle: The scriptures always and everywhere speak primarily of God, and only secondarily and derivatively about us. Scripture has theology as its primary intent rather than anthropology. We begin looking for God before we look for us. Or rather, we affirm that God began, in Jesus Christ, looking for us before we ever looked for God.

In service to the congregation, we preachers attempt to listen to the Word, expecting to hear about God. Then, after our study, we ask God for the courage to speak about God to our people. All revitalization of the church begins here because the church is of God.

Sermon Outline

Monday morning: Think about what went wrong with yesterday's sermon. Make vow never to preach from Leviticus again. Call the man who felt that my reference to the "need for strong and visionary leadership" was a cheap shot at George Bush. Play eighteen holes of golf.

Tuesday afternoon: Try to get up the nerve to look at next Sunday's lessons. Watch *Love Boat* reruns instead. What did C. H. Spurgeon do on Tuesdays? Write to the man who thought I slurred President Bush. Tell him I was referring to Moses.

Wednesday morning: Oh, great. It's the prodigal son again. Why didn't the bishop move me last year? I've done it from the father's perspective, the younger brother's point of view, the older brother's side. I'm desperate for new material. Thumb through back issues of *Field and Stream,* looking for new illustrations.

Thursday, all day: Search for commentaries on Luke. Can find only two in my possession—one by a post-Bultmannian, the other by the guy who gave me a C minus in New Testament 103. Spend rest of afternoon thumbing through back issues of *The Christian Ministry*. Why doesn't anybody preach on the prodigal son anymore?

Friday morning: Only a fool would preach on the prodigal son. Today, I must get something down on paper: "Why do we all enjoy watching reruns on TV? *Gilligan's Island* is as funny today as it was when I was a kid. Is *Silas Marner* any less of a classic just because you read it in high school? So it is with many familiar biblical stories." What a beginning! That'll grab 'em. I'm rolling at last!

Saturday night: I've cut the *Silas Marner* opener. I hated the book when I was seventeen, and wouldn't read it again even if someone held a gun to my head. It's the midnight hour. Put-up or shut-up time for the preacher. Do or die. Who says we've got to have a sermon *every* Sunday? Perhaps I could read from the latest *Time* editorial and we could break up into buzz groups. No. That would work only in California. Why can't my church be in California?

Sunday morning: Personally, I thought it all went quite well. I work best under pressure. About 2:00 in the morning the juices really started flowing. Minimal feedback from the pews except for a rather snide, "Well, aren't we creative? I don't recall ever before hearing Luke 15:11-32 from the perspective of the fatted calf."

Monday morning: The trouble with these people is that they don't know an artistic sermon when they hear one. When will we be done with Luke? Hurry, Advent. Call the woman who complained about the Barbara Bush joke. Tomorrow I'll see what's on deck for next Sunday's lessons. Play eighteen holes of golf.

Section 2 | People Who Are Pastors

The Perils of *Not* Passing By on the Other Side

WE WERE COMING OUT OF THE DINER, MY FRIEND and I, he a preacher and I one too. Heading down the street toward our churches, we came across a poor old man sprawled out on the edge of the sidewalk, head swirling around in drunken stupor.

A man was going down from Jerusalem to Jericho, and fell into the hands of robbers. . . . Now by chance a priest was going down that road; and when he saw him, he passed by on the other side. . . .

"Poor old man," said my friend.

"You know, we really ought to do something," said I. "He could get hurt out here in his condition."

"After all, we're in the business, right?" said my friend.

"Yea, right," said I. That's how it started.

But a Samaritan while traveling came near him; and when he saw him, he was moved with pity. He went to him and bandaged his wounds, having poured oil and wine on them.

My friend took one of the man's arms, and I took the other. With some difficulty, we got him to his feet. He was dressed in a rumpled, terribly dirty old suit, with a crumpled hat. As he attempted to steady himself, he swerved and staggered back and forth on the sidewalk, my friend and I staggering with him, trying to get him upright.

"Easy does it," the man mumbled. "Look out for those slippery places!"

"Hey, old man, you really ought to get some help," said my friend. The three of us, the man with my friend and I on either side, staggered and tottered down the sidewalk, people scurrying out of our way.

"Where do we take someone in this condition?" I wondered aloud.

"There's got to be somewhere for people like him," said my friend.

"Would you mind what you're doing," said the old man in an aggravated tone of voice, "you're going to run aground and kill everybody on the boat!"

We staggered and tottered, the three of us, to a nearby phone booth.

My friend left me outside to wrestle with the recipient of our compassion while my friend began thumbing through the phone book. "Well, are we going to just stand here, or are we going to go inside and eat lunch?" asked the man, gesturing toward the phone booth.

"Aha! Here we are, the Greenville Alcohol Information Center," said my friend. "It's not too far from here. We can drive it in five minutes."

We staggered, the three of us, on down the street, with the man mumbling, "What was wrong with that restaurant? It looked good to me."

Then he put him on his own animal, brought him to an inn, and took care of him.

Once in my friend's car—he in the front, and me and our ward in the back—we headed toward the Alcohol Information Center. By the time we reached Main Street, the old man had passed out again and was snoring quietly on my shoulder.

Just after we turned on to busy Main Street, without warning, the old man began to shout, curse, and kick.

"Hold him!" said my friend, looking over into the backseat where I was wrestling for all that I was worth. The man was kicking, screaming something about "Snakes, everywhere, snakes!"

With that he somehow managed to kick the back door open and fell forward out of the car and into the street. The car stopped. All I had to hold him in the car was the seat of his pants, pants which, with his struggling to get away and my struggling to hold him, were now being pulled down to his hips.

"Help me!" he began shouting to the people on the sidewalk. "Help me! I don't even know these people and they are trying to take me someplace! Help!"

There I was—traffic stopped in the middle of Main Street—attempting to wrestle this old man back into the car while also speaking to the now gathering crowd on the street: "I am a Methodist. My friend is a Baptist. We are clergy. We are helping this old man here."

"I don't want no help from nobody, 'specially no preachers!" he was shouting to the crowd.

I finally succeeded in forcing him back into the backseat, and the car sped away. After a few more moments of struggle, the old man passed out once again and slept peacefully until we arrived at the big office building that housed the Alcohol Information Center.

It wasn't easy getting a totally unconscious man out of the car, across the street, into the lobby, on the elevator, and up to the ninth floor. I had him propped up in one corner of the elevator, where he kept sliding to the floor.

"I am a Methodist minister," I kept saying to people who got on the elevator. "We are helping this man. My friend is a Baptist."

The Alcohol Information Center consisted of a young woman seated behind a desk. On the desk were stacks of leaflets about substance abuse. That was it. When the three of us staggered into her office, it was obvious that she had never actually seen an inebriated person in her life, probably never seen two clergy, either.

"You can't bring him in here," she said to us.

"But he needs help," protested my friend.

"Not here," she said. When he persisted, she agreed to go upstairs and ask her boss what we might do with the man (who now slept in one of the metal chairs, his head resting peacefully on her desk between the stacks of pamphlets).

The next day he took out two denarii, gave them to the innkeeper, and said, "Take care of him; and when I come back, I will repay you whatever more you spend."

As soon as she left the office my friend and I looked at one another and, without a word of deliberation, quietly but quickly tiptoed out of the office and ran for the elevator, leaving the recipient of our good will sleeping between stacks of pamphlets.

Once downstairs and on the street, we sped away, he to work on next Sunday's sermon, me to the tennis court.

Luke 10:29-37. Easier to preach than to practice.

Pastoral Pugilism

(With gratitude to James Thurber)

Teaching, as I do, at a mainline Protestant seminary, I am often asked, particularly by young seminarians, to enunciate hard and fast rules for pastoral work. Impressed as they are by the complex demands of the pastoral ministry, seminarians are always seeking some means of simplification. They persist in asking, "Do you think it is *always* wrong to perform a marriage at a nudist colony?" Others will demand, "Professor, wouldn't it *always* be a bad idea to use tape recorded sound effects in a sermon?"

Alas, for these meager ministerial minds, pastoral work is complex, requiring constant exercise of mature, theologically informed pastoral judgment. After twenty years of being a pastor, I can tell you that there are few things that I would never, always, or habitually do or not do. While I cannot defend Situational Ethics theologically, I can certainly defend it experientially and pastorally. As a pastor, one simply must take things, and people, as they come.

For instance, I have met pastors—generally conservative traditionalists, but not always—who doggedly maintain that it is "always wrong to strike a parishioner." These tend to be the same people who feel that it is always wrong to use a comma splice within a sentence, or to begin or end a homily with the phrase, "You idiots."

Even though such sentimental and archaic notions die slowly, every pastor I know who has enjoyed more than a decade in the pastoral ministry will recall a layperson who, on one ecclesial occasion or another, has to be slugged in the jaw.

I recall, for instance, a layman of my acquaintance, a leader in one of my early congregations who during formal worship services had an inclination to hum. Perhaps one hymn would remind him of another. Or some said that he hummed as a protest against the "high church" hymn, which the organist and I had selected for the occasion. The hymns he hummed tended always to be evangelical ditties. A helpful layperson, seeing the dilemma that this man put me in, would nudge him with his elbow. When this failed, a particularly supportive older woman pinched him; still he hummed. I was forced, as conscientious pastors often are, to take matters in hand during a Christmas Eve service last year. I found that a sharp, downward blow upon his neck, smartly given, would render him into a sort of happy stupor. We had no problem with him for the remainder of the service. When he came forward for communion, he had a rather beatific smile upon his face and was most placid and receptive. He was really quite charming after that.

I know what you are thinking. A pastor who is unaware of his or her own strength could deliver a blow to a parishioner with a bit too much enthusiasm, thus helping the slugged parishioner beyond the beatific vision into lying out cold under the pew. This result is likely to prove offensive to other worshipers and, of course, ought to be avoided if at all possible. It is important not to hinder the free flow of traffic in and out of pews during a service.

Now, I have known pastors, usually those of a somewhat delicate disposition, who, to avoid overshooting the mark in striking a parishioner, would sometimes, say, during a discussion at a board meeting, merely shove the parishioner backward. They hoped thereby to achieve the needed result of silencing the offending parishioner. While restraint of force has its benefits, one of my friends, during a debate related to the annual church budget, shoved a particularly difficult man backward over a folding chair, landing him in the lap of a woman who, prior to that moment, had been one of the pastor's most ardent supporters. Sometimes direct, swift force is much more effective than the timid shove.

On the other hand, though a swift blow to the head, or even the back of the neck, can be extremely effective in the long run, sometimes the affected person has a tendency to shout. While this is moderately disruptive in services of worship, it can be disastrous in church business meetings when the shout elicited thereby only serves to increase the emotional temperature of the meeting. As I have found, shouting at meetings sometimes leads to people throwing things, to others jumping on tables, and similar unfortunate side effects.

I, as much as the next person, hate to see church meetings end in a brawl. However, I find it surprising how even the most staid congregation will degenerate into hysterics when something is thrown during a service of worship—say, a piece of furniture, a fixture of altarware, a hymnal, or a purse. What is there about the human species that infects it with a seemingly overwhelming desire to join in the fray once something is thrown? Undoubtedly, Calvin discussed this propensity somewhere in his *Institutes,* though I, by the date of this publication, have been unable to locate it.

Of course, during some worship service everybody has had the urge to throw a hymnal at someone. In my experience, this tendency is evoked most frequently by church musicians. However, speakers from the Gideons, those giving testimonials on "Youth Sunday," as well as representatives of the presiding bishop, also appear to have this effect on me. While many laypersons, apathetic lot that they are, can be made to resist such a tendency, even the most jaded and morose congregation can be moved into action with a hymnal or attendance registration pad being thrown at the right moment in a service. Even the most apathetic church member, even the most casual and sporadic church attender finds it difficult to sit by once a few hymnals are thrown at an offensive organist. This sudden burst of enthusiasm appears to be engendered not only by the excitement of sailing objects and their attendant crashes, but also by the gleeful shouts of "Gotcha!" and "How do you like that?"

Eventually, someone is bound to be knocked out cold by a poorly aimed hymnal, or a folding metal church chair improperly tossed. These things happen. It is impossible for a pastor to please everybody. My advice on these occasions is to offer apologies. Let there be consideration of whether or not the coldcocked parishioner *deserved* to be knocked out cold. Then continue with the service, the meeting, or the discussion after the wounded party has been discreetly dragged away.

Those who quote paragraph numbers from *The United Methodist Book of Discipline* in response to a pastor's proposal—people who in an argument quote from obscure passages of Scripture, saying, "That may be true, pastor, but of course, you also know the advice in Obadiah 1:4 . . ."—earn themselves the right to be hit with a folding metal church chair. No one ever quotes Scripture to a pastor without a desire to embarrass and belittle.

I also recall the man who, in a particularly difficult meeting, asked me, "Did they teach you stuff like this in seminary?" Naturally, this query begged for a sharp right thrust to the side of his jaw.

Against such pastoral care, I know of no biblical prohibition.

The Extravagant Vocation

A few years ago, Bishop Fred Borsch published a book on the parables of Jesus, calling many of them "parables of extravagance." So many of Jesus' parables, according to Borsch, speak of extravagance and waste.

The disciples said to Jesus, "Show us the Father." And in response, he portrayed an extravagant, divine effusiveness at the very heart of reality:

A farmer went out to sow. Did he carefully prepare the soil, removing all rocks and weeds, mark off neat rows, place each seed exactly six inches from the other, and cover each with three-quarters an inch of soil?

No. This sower just began slinging seed. Seed everywhere.

Some fell on the path, some on rocks and in weeds, and some, miraculously, fell on good soil, took root, and rendered harvest. That's sort of what the Word of God is like, said Jesus.

A farmer (I think it was the same farmer) had a field. The servants came running in breathlessly: "Master, there are weeds coming up in the midst of your new wheat."

"An enemy must have done this!" cried the farmer.

Enemy, my eye. You get this sort of agricultural mess when you sow seed with such abandon.

"Do you want us to go out and carefully root up those weeds from your good wheat?" asked the servants.

"No, let 'em grow. I just live to see stuff grow. We'll sort it all out in September."

And Jesus said God runs God's kingdom like that.

In this kingdom belongs the woman who tore her living room apart until she found her stray quarter; a father who plows ten grand into a welcome-home party for a prodigal; and a shepherd called "good" for his willingness to lay down his life for a $3.95, plus postage, sheep.

Anyone called in service to this God had better be in the business of extravagance, wasteful effusiveness. Bean counters, accountants of all kinds, misers, and anal-retentive types bore this God. The best pastors I know are the most messy, those who don't mind wasting a little time with people, throwing away a few words in service to a kingdom without bounds.

Speaking at the Princeton Theological Seminary graduation last year, I congratulated these Presbyterians for their mastery of Greek and Hebrew. Not that such knowledge will be of any utility to them in their future parish ministry. You can't use Greek to build a "megachurch," nor will it fold out into a bed, nor can it be used to dice julienne fries. We make them learn Greek not because it has anything to do with "successful" Christian ministry, but in the hope that we will thereby render them so impractical that, having wasted so much time with a dead language, they may not balk at wasting an afternoon with an eighty-year-old nursing home resident or at spending a Saturday listening to the life of a troubled teenager.

"She could have gone to law school. Best undergraduate I ever taught," he said as we veered off the main highway and made our way down a narrow country road in West Virginia. At last we pulled up before the little white frame Presbyterian church whose sign, peeling paint and hanging from a rusted chain had the name of the church and underneath, painted poorly, "The Rev. Julie Jones—Pastor."

And my friend said, "What a waste."

But the reckless farmer who slung the seed, and the woman who pulled up her carpet and moved the living-room furniture into the yard in pursuit of her lost quarter, and the shepherd who threw away his life for the sheep laughed with disordered delight.

Practical Theology

Most of the seminary courses I have taught come under the heading of "practical theology"—courses like church administration, preaching, and counseling. Many people feel that we ought to offer even more of these practical, down-to-earth, "how-to-do-it" classes rather than so many "theoretical" subjects like church history, systematic theology, Greek, Hebrew, and ethics.

"Your graduates know a lot of abstractions about ministry," a church official told me, "but they are unschooled in how to be ministers." It seems ridiculous to him that people should emerge from seminary knowing about Augustine, Teresa of Avila, and Karl Barth, but ignorant about how to conduct a stewardship program. I see his point. And yet, parish ministry has a way of making the most impractical subjects practical.

Scarcely two years out of seminary, I was amazed at how impractical many of the courses in so-called practical theology actually were. My course in church administration had taught me how to build a new sanctuary, which I've never had the opportunity to do. My semester of United Methodist polity was rendered irrelevant by two weeks of legislation at General Conference.

On the other hand, boring old church history proved to be shockingly practical. I faced a congregation of people who thought they were Georgian Methodists but who were actually Hindus, Buddhists, pantheists, Docetists, or followers of some other heresies and religions that even Roland Bainton had never heard of. Though I didn't feel compelled to tell them that the church had tried their theology back in the fourth century and had found it wanting, it made all the difference to me to be able to name their theologies.

What we most need, twenty years into the pastorate, is not new ways of conducting stewardship campaigns, but reminders of why we are here in this sea of trivial, accommodationist congregational demands. What we need is some means of focusing on the utterly essential beyond the merely important. A tough class in the history of doctrine may keep us on course in the face of cultural demands that we forsake Christian ministry and do something useful.

A friend who is now a full-time pastoral counselor used to make fun of my interest in reading theology. In seminary, he was all Carl Rogers to my John Wesley. The other day we had a long, rather surprising, conversation about Barth's view of revelation and experience.

"What is this?" I asked. "I thought you believed theology began and ended with Carl Rogers."

"That was yesterday," he replied. "When I was in my twenties, setting out to make people well, I had no need of such abstraction. Today it's different."

I asked him what was different.

"When you listen to the expression of raw human need, eight hours a day, five days a week, you need something beyond the practical. You need something to keep you from drowning. You need some means of transcending others' pleas for help and your own desire to be helpful."

Recently I had a tough week. Everything went wrong. Finally, I took Friday off and read through nearly all of Thomas Oden's volume of systematic theology, *The Word of Life*. It was one of the most useless, impractical books I have read in a long time. Nothing in it helped me to do practical tasks.

However, the next day, when someone called me "pastor," I

liked the sound of it and knew she was speaking to me. No small gift from five hundred pages of theology.

Be Imitators of Me

"Be imitators of me," says Paul. "You have a worthy example in us." So Paul advises the Corinthians, the Thessalonians, and the Galatians. "Become as I am," he tells them. Is there no limit to apostolic presumption?

Picture this: Would I begin a homiletics class by saying, "The goal of this class is for you to imitate me"?

No. It strikes us as the height of conceit.

What I say is, "Class, I'm going to lay out a few principles, a few interesting ideas—though not my own—and some insights for discussion, then I want you to make up your mind. You see, I respect your identity, your individuality. I don't want to force myself on you or to make you my disciples."

What this really means is, "I want to get through this class without taking responsibility for your life. Stay out of my life, and I'll promise to stay out of yours."

At a faculty retreat a few years ago, one of my colleagues asked, "Does it bother any of you that some of our students are sexually promiscuous, that some are indulging in self-destructive and addictive practices?"

Well, we said, we must respect their privacy. What we meant was, God forbid that we should hold our students accountable for not only what they know but who they are. If we did that, you know what might happen? They might turn and hold us accountable, speak the truth to us about our lifestyles, personal habits, and inconsistencies.

In appealing to his flock for imitation, Paul was placing himself squarely within that moral and pedagogical tradition that asserted that the purpose of learning is imitation of the master, that teachers have a responsibility to live as they teach, to walk as they speak, and that pupils are challenged not only to learn but also to be transformed.

The Enlightenment taught us that anybody can be good simply by thinking clearly, by using reason, common sense, or other individualistic attributes and natural endowments, which allegedly reside in everybody, regardless of that person's background.

This view of goodness was counter to that offered by moralists like Aristotle, who taught that goodness was essentially a matter not of being reasonable or of making right choices, but rather of being trained to be good. One must be taught how to be good. Aristotle's chief analogy for learning morality was learning to ride a horse. A person can't learn to ride a horse by reading a book, or by having parents who know how to ride a horse. One learns to ride a horse by watching someone who is good at riding, by being led step-by-step by that person, and by imitating her moves.

For the little band of Christians at Philippi, constantly in danger of seduction by the majority pagan culture, there was no better textbook than the lives of those who bore the burden of leadership. Discipleship still depends on identifying examples, saints, people worthy of imitation.

If every hundred years or so we cannot point to a Teresa of Calcutta, a Martin Luther King, Jr., a Desmond Tutu, or even good old Pastor Brown, then we have a problem, because the world is quite right in judging Christianity by the lives it produces. Lacking changed lives, we pervert the gospel into a cerebral exercise. But Christianity is a lifestyle, the following of someone headed in a direction one would not normally go.

I'm a pastor. My congregation is right to expect a congruence between what I preach and the way I live. So go ahead, I say to my people, imitate me. Demand that my life be a worthy example. Don't let me off the discipleship hook. Insist that I preach by the way I walk, rather than merely by the Book. They might make a pastor out of me yet.

Busy Pastors

He is a busy pastor. His six-hundred-member congregation keeps him jumping. Fifteen hours a week in pastoral counseling, three hospitals to be visited, and more than a dozen nursing homes. Then there is the Sunday service and sermon, a young adult Bible study class on Sunday morning, the Confirmation Classes in the spring. Add to these parochial duties the presidency of the local ministerial association, and active in Rotary, Urban League, and United Way. He is a very busy, fifty-hours-a-week, active, conscientious, committed—alas, utterly empty and now at fifty—vacuous pastor. His body is there—in the pulpit, at the bedside, in the board meeting—but not the eyes, whence the gleam has gone. Not the soul.

The first time I went to my church's annual conference, when I was fresh out of seminary, was my first encounter with them—back-slapping, hand-shaking, loud-talking, burned-out hulks. Where once there had been caring, believing, vibrant pastors, now no one was home. And I felt fear, knowing that I was no better than they, knowing that I was probably a good deal more capable than they of beginning ministry by giving to others and ending ministry having given away the store, sold the farm, spiritually speaking. When would I, shorn of youthful enthusiasm, divested of vision, look just like them?

Is not this the danger of which Henri Nouwen warned us in saying, "If pastors are uncertain of what is absolutely essential in ministry, they tend to lose themselves in the merely important"?

How well that describes our pastoral dilemma. It is important to visit in the hospital. It is valuable for a pastor to be active in community affairs. No one questions the significance of our study and preparation to preach and to lead worship. Yet even such important business as this can degenerate into busyness. The intellectual, emotional, spiritual demands of the parish ministry are so great that it is easy for pastors to become distracted into areas that are important but not essential. If you leave me to my devices, I will take longer to open my morning mail than for my morning prayer. So dismal are my failures at meeting God, I am grateful to substitute meetings with committees. I go to meetings, therefore, I am. My fatigue is irrefutable evidence for my fidelity. Everybody is saved by grace but the pastor.

As usual, the great P. T. Forsyth said it better than I:

"It is possible to be so active in the service of Christ as to forget to love him. Many preach Christ but get in front of him by the multiplicity of their own works. It will be your ruin if you do! Christ can do without your works; what he wants is you. Yet if he really has you he will have all your works."

Can I dare to believe the validity of my vocation? Can I embrace, on a daily basis, the continuing scandal that God, for reasons known only to God, called *me,* wants me even more than my works, wants me so that my works might be, not as of my own devising but as gracious by-products of my having been called, named, owned by God? How can I keep remembering that the sum of my pastoral actions as much busyness is less important than my actions as my response to God's graciousness?

Dear God, forgive me for being so active in serving you that I forget to love you. Amen.

I Was Vanna's Pastor

The other day I was standing in the supermarket checkout line, madly perusing the latest *Star* magazine in an attempt to finish the article "Vanna Says Nude Photo Is Cheap Shot" before I arrived at the cash register. The woman behind me bumped me with her cart and said, "Either move up in line and pay for it like everybody else, buddy, or let me by."

I turned and said to her in an indignant tone, "Madam, I'll have you know that you are addressing Vanna White's former pastor."

She shrieked, and then asked for my autograph. Everything came to a halt in the supermarket as people crowded around me. Before it was all over, the manager had given me a free copy of the *Star* after I promised always to shop at his store.

Although the *Star* doesn't report it, and you probably will not read about it in her new, long-awaited and hot autobiography, *Vanna Speaks*, it is true: *I was Vanna White's pastor.* The glamorous but taciturn beauty who turns letters on *Wheel of Fortune* was a leader in my church's youth group in North Myrtle Beach, South Carolina.

I admit that I can't exactly detect the influence of my preaching when I watch Vanna turn her letters on *Wheel of Fortune*. About the most they let Vanna say about theology is, "Big money! Big money!" But I am sure that my stamp is there, however subtly.

I expect that her autobiography will contain no mention of my ministerial influence. When David Letterman asked Vanna about the most interesting men she has met, she mentioned only Merv Griffin and Tom Selleck. Perhaps she has forgotten my powerful sermons, or the fascinating course on "Christian Sex, Dating, and Marriage" I gave the youth every year.

Perhaps.

Perhaps Vanna never speaks about me because she remembers the advice I gave her. One Sunday in May of her senior year at North Myrtle Beach High, I asked, "Vanna, what are you planning after graduation?" She replied, in her unfailingly sweet and sincere way, that she had always dreamed of going into modeling, so she was going to modeling school in Atlanta.

"Vanna, no!" I said. (I flunked nondirective counseling in seminary.) "Don't do that! Those schools will do nothing but take your money. Nobody ever gets a job at one of those places. You have brains! Ability! You could be more than a model!"

She thanked me politely and said, "But I have this dream of going to Hollywood and becoming an actress."

"From North Myrtle Beach?" I asked. "Vanna, that only happens in movies. This is crazy!"

According to the *Star*, Vanna makes more in two days of taping *Wheel of Fortune* than I make in a whole year of giving good advice to aspiring teenagers.

Just Say No

Some pastors find it utterly impossible to say no. The word is not in their clerical vocabulary, the sad result of Tillichian acceptance of their acceptance, accepting everything gone wild, I suppose. Oh, they mean and want to say no, but someone—a parishioner, a bishop, the president of the PTA—will say, "Oh, please don't refuse us. It won't take much of your time. Besides, everyone else is *working*."

Then begins the pitiful process of self-doubt, insecurity, and the general ministerial desire to please, leading to the inevitable. "Well, I suppose I could, just this once. What harm would it do? It might even do some good, and I so want to do good."

I think the pastor with the worst case of this was the Reverend Adrian Smollett, who served my Aunt Agnes's church. He shouldn't have gone there; he knew he would be miserable, but the bishop called and Smollett couldn't refuse. From the day he arrived, the congregation quickly realized that Smollett was an easy mark. At his past church, Smollett's damning agreeableness had brought him, and the congregation, to grief. He had resolved not to let it happen here. But scarcely had he unpacked his belongings when the trouble began.

"I want you to visit with me at Rotary," said the chairperson of the administrative board. Smollett had his fill of civic clubs, with their brooms, pancakes, and booths at football games, at his previous post and therefore replied, "Thank you. It's nice of you to ask, and I do want to be active in the community. But I like to keep my lunch hour open."

"Come now, man," said his tormentor, "surely you can't be busy every day at noon." Smollett was too polite to lie and too full of grace to say no. He capitulated. He was now not only a Methodist but also a Rotarian.

But then what was he to say to other church members who invited him to Civitan, Lions, Ruritan, and the Full Gospel Business Men's Fellowship? Smollett said yes to them all. As a result, he took only two meals a week with his family. He was always brimming with English peas, sliced turkey, and misery.

But eventually Smollett's fatal flaw caught up with him. The church officers didn't balk when he took over every job in the church. ("Quite a go-getter we have for a preacher," they would brag in town.) But they began to take a more critical look at Smollett's ministry among them. Many opposed the color he painted the church fellowship hall. Actually, Smollett couldn't be blamed for the final result. Someone mentioned how much money the church could save by doing the job themselves, and Smollett, true to form, grabbed a brush and got busy. Unfortunately, he used leftover paint from the hardware store, and the fellowship hall got painted half peach and half OSHA-approved orange.

He also performed at least six weddings a day and ten funerals a week, at least half of which were for Buddhists, Muslims, and an assortment of people who believe in Shirley MacLaine.

His end came not from overwork and fatigue, as everyone predicted, but from an infected cat bite he received at the St. Francis Day Blessing of the Animals Service. On the day he died, he went in and out of consciousness, alert just long enough to marry a couple who were passing through town on their way to Atlanta. He also addressed the weekly luncheon of nursing students by way of the hospital's closed-circuit TV system.

Toward the end, he raved incoherently, "Yes . . . that is, I suppose that I could . . . No, I'm not all that busy today . . . Yes, more peas, please . . . It is a pleasure to be here this evening . . . I don't really mind." Then, he breathed his last.

His soul was seen trudging toward that place of eternal bliss, resigned yet confident that it would be granted divine affirmation.

Influence Incognito

Much of the good that you do as a pastor is incognito, unknown to you though not to the recipient of your beneficence. When my mentor Carlyle Marney died, I wrote a tribute to him in *The Christian Century*. Among the letters I received, one from a fellow pastor, said, "Marney was instrumental in three of the major shifts in my life—yet I never met him and he was unaware of his deep influence upon me."

When pastors complain that we are ineffective or frustrated by lack of response to our ministry, we ought to be reminded that we are probably the least capable of judging such matters. Some of our most powerful effects upon others are unknown to us.

Though you haven't, if you were to ask me to name one of the greatest influences upon my ministry, it would be the teaching of a crusty old professor at Yale Divinity School, though to this moment he knew nothing of his gift to me.

With great trepidation I took his legendary course in Kierkegaard.

"Whatever you do, don't dare ask a question. He hates that," advised a seasoned senior. The first lecture was brilliant. At the end, the professor asked, "Questions?"

Some student, in a foolhardy attempt to impress, stood and offered a longish, pedantic dissertation disguised as a question. At the end, the professor looked at the student for an eternal minute and then said, "Any other questions?"

That was the end of that.

The course was great. All that I expected. Abrasive, passionate, cynical, ironic; it wasn't *about* Kierkegaard. It was Kierkegaard doing Kierkegaard doing the gospel.

Later in the semester, shortly after we had submitted our papers (I had cancelled everything in order to devote full time to research my "Kierkegaard on Preaching"), the professor ended a class with his usual "Questions?" Of course there were none. How dumb do we look? Then, looking out over the class, he asked, "Willimon? Who is Willimon?"

I raised a trembling hand.

"See me sometime this afternoon," he said as he whisked out the door.

I sat in stunned terror. Was the paper that bad? All right, so I might have muffed a reference or two, but I spent a lot of time on it. That ought to count for something.

All afternoon I rehearsed in my mind various scenarios. The professor asking me to rewrite the paper and I compliantly agreeing. He asking me to drop the course and I asking to go quietly. He flunking me and I appealing to his Lutheran sense of unmerited grace.

At 3:00 I tapped on his office door. I entered. I took a seat.

The professor muttered, "Fools. I work with such ineptitude."

This was not a promising beginning. The best I could hope for was a WP.

He gestured toward a stack of papers. "Most of them rubbish. Where are you from?" he asked.

I replied.

"That explains nothing," he said out of the side of his mouth.

"Your paper," he said. "Your paper moved me almost to tears."

That bad? To my consternation, I recalled that Lutherans are also high on Law.

"So well stated, understated, well said. Really quite remarkable writing, quite unusual amid the refuse that passes for scholarly writing today."

"Really?" I asked in wonderment. "Well, er, uh, thanks. I'm glad you liked it."

"Of course, typically weak on content," he continued. "Yet so well said, I hardly noticed."

The medium really is the message, I thought.

"You must develop your talent. That is all."

I soared across the quadrangle; sailed; composed books, articles, various monographs as I flew, sent aloft by a man who never wasted words. I could write.

Years later, seven to be exact, the same professor was giving a lecture at Duke, a guest of the Department of Philosophy. I waited in the vestibule to greet him. He entered. I approached him, saying, "Professor, remember me? I took your Kierkegaard course. Now I'm here on the faculty at Duke Divinity School."

He looked at me blankly.

Now nervous, I said, "Wrote the paper on Kierkegaard and preaching. You, er, liked it. At least you liked the writing."

As he continued into the auditorium, he glanced toward me and said, "No, I don't remember."

To Tell the Truth

Leaning down toward the bottom shelf to retrieve his trusty *Strong's*, pursuing "new moon" through both Testaments, the

Reverend Henry Henderson, for the past five years pastor of Sword of Truth Presbyterian Church, bumped his head.

"Darn," he exclaimed to himself, grabbing his stunned forehead.

This he followed immediately with "Damn," muttered with atypical candor. The rather non-ministerial ejaculation surprised Henderson. He could hardly believe he said it. "Damn," he heard himself say again. "Damn, this hurts."

That, so far as the Reverend Henderson could tell, was how it all began—an accidental blow to the brain while in the act of reaching for a concordance.

Moments later the phone rang. "Pastor," whined a nasal voice at the other end, "are you busy?"

"Not at all," said Henderson out of habit to the voice on the other end of the line. Then, from nowhere, Henderson said, "I'm sitting here in my study just dying for someone like you to call and make my day! No, I *am* busy. I was working on my sermon for next Sunday. What is it?"

His words paralyzed him. They must have also stunned the whining voice at the other end of the line, for there was a long, awkward silence followed by, "Er, well, I can call back. I'll call you at home tonight after work, Pastor."

"No," Henderson said firmly, alien words forming in his mouth as if not by his own devising, "call me during office hours on any day other than Friday. Thank you. Goodbye."

The receiver dropped from his hand and into the telephone cradle. He felt odd. Yes, quite odd. His head no longer throbbed. Yet he felt odd.

Emerging from his study, he encountered Jane Smith, who had come to church on her usual Friday duties for the Altar Guild. "As usual, just me," she said to Henderson. "They all *say* they'll be on the Guild, that they don't mind helping out the church. Yet, when it comes time for the work, where are they?"

"I think you know very well why they are not here," said Henderson. "You gave them only a half-hearted invitation. Everyone knows you love playing the martyr. Their absence helps bolster your holier-than-thou attitude."

Smith nearly dropped the offering plate she was holding, along with the polishing cloth and polish. "Pastor! How dare you accuse me of being a complainer! You know how hard I've worked to get the Altar Guild going! If you gave us volunteers the kind of support we ought to . . ."

Henderson wasn't listening. He was staggering down the hall as Jane Smith continued her complaint. He was feeling dizzy, unsteady.

Out in the parking lot, gasping for fresh air, Henderson was spied by John Tyler.

"Glad I caught you," said Tyler. "Pray for Florence. She's under the weather again. Just working herself to death, I think. She won't be at the Finance Committee meeting tonight. I'll tell her I told you."

"I doubt that Florence will know whether you told me or not, considering her condition," said Henderson to Tyler.

"What do you mean?" asked Tyler.

"You know what I mean. 'Under the weather' is your euphemistic way of saying 'dead drunk.' Denial is not just a river in Egypt, John. I've tried to broach the subject with you and Florence before. When you're ready to face the truth about Florence's habit, let me know. Until then, spare me the excuses."

Henderson got into his blue Toyota and shut the door, leaving Tyler staring dumbly at him from the church walk. Seated behind the steering wheel, Henderson started the car, backing it out quickly, as if he knew where he was going and what he was doing. He didn't. He was a man losing control. He simply could not not tell the truth, no matter how much he wanted to do otherwise.

He was a pastor in peril.

Henderson at the hospital that afternoon, Room 344: "So the doctor tells you your heart problems are congenital? That so? Are you sure the doctor didn't mention anything about (by my reckoning) *80 pounds of excess fat?*"

And in Room 204: "Really? So this is the strain of emphysema that is not caused by smoking? Give me a break! Get real! Two packs a day for thirty years and you wonder why you're sucking on an oxygen tank for dear life?"

Henderson at the Finance Committee meeting that evening: "Why wring our hands about the sad state of the budget? Don't need to be Einstein to figure this one out. I know very well that I am giving more to this church than anybody in the room tonight, and *you* know that I've got the lowest salary of anyone in the room—thanks to you. George, I don't expect you to be a tither, but don't you feel a bit guilty weighing in at only 2 or 3 percent of your income—*after* taxes?"

In teaching the young people's Bible class that Sunday, Henderson was reported to have told them, "There are reasons for thinking that Paul never wrote 2 Corinthians—though most of us preachers are cunning enough never to tell you about the textual problems. I've always thought that Paul probably did write most of it, considering some of the screwy ideas therein, which sound to me like Paul on one of his bad days."

His last words to the frantic choir director, just before the procession began, were, or so it was said, "Why worry about not having a couple of tenors? Will tenors redeem an anthem already ravaged and despoiled by this choir?"

In that fateful Sunday's service—after a pastoral prayer in which Henderson admitted to God that "Most of us didn't really want to be here today, least of all to hear anything truthful you have to reveal to us," followed by a sermon in which Henderson asserted, "While the prophet Amos does not identify these 'fat cows of Bashan,' I could name a few right here in this congregation," and "I daresay most of you here today have been brought here more by your desire to polish your idealized self-image than to worship the living God"—an emergency meeting of the Pastor/Parish Committee was called. Of course, Henderson was fired, or at least that was what Henderson afterward said the committee did to him. The committee officially stated that, "In a show of Christian compassion and concern, we are offering Brother Henderson a month's worth of free counseling and rest so that he can ponder where the Lord will lead him next. We pray for him and wish him God's blessings in his new field of ministry—wherever that may be."

The now former Reverend Henderson would later claim, "That

bump on the head made a prophet out of me, despite myself."
Most members of Sword of Truth Church, for compassion's sake,
never spoke his name in years to come. When Henderson's name
was mentioned, someone would always ask, "Wasn't that the poor
man who suddenly went kinda crazy?"

Section 3 | Worship

Give of Your Best to the Master

I WISH YOU COULD HAVE KNOWN HELENA PITTS. For at least thirty years she presided over (more accurately, tyrannized) the Broad Street United Methodist Church Altar Guild. Helena felt strongly that if it's worth doing for God it is worth doing right. "Right" meant perfectly polished altarware every Sunday, acolytes in pressed albs wearing white gloves (the young male acolytes hated those gloves, but none of the young hooligans had the temerity to resist Miss Helena on the issue of gloves).

I recall vividly the Sunday after Epiphany when, as clergy and choir were going outside, Helena, fire in her eye, came tearing out of the sanctuary commanding the clergy, "Hold everything! Some fool thinks we're still Green when it's the first Sunday in Lent." We waited until Helena had set things right.

By some accounts Helena was fastidious, fussy, and compulsive about the setting for Sunday worship, and many is the time I've been grateful—with my wrinkled alb stuffed between a poorly tied cincture—that I'm at a church far from Helena's critical liturgical gaze.

Here at Duke Chapel I tire of the every Monday "M and M Meetings." Here, for over an hour, we ministers and musicians meet and evaluate yesterday's service. Usually that's something like, "When did you think the service died, before the sermon, or after?"

I tire of agonizing over the spacing in the draft of the bulletin;

73

I get fatigued with our protracted debate over whether a hymn is fitting or not. Musicians, particularly the anal-retentive type, get on my nerves.

Last Sunday I met a couple who told me that they drive over thirty miles every Sunday to worship with us. When I asked, "Why on earth would you do that?" they replied, "We're picky about how we praise God."

I asked them to explain, and he said, "We are both in demanding jobs. We are busy people. When we come to worship, we have great needs, great expectations. To be met by a pastor who appears to have slept in the robe he is wearing, to be given a bulletin that was used to clean the mimeograph machine, to be subjected to a choir who has just seen the music, and a pastor who was too self-consumed to do us the favor of preparing is an affront."

Well, you can see their point. The casually formed service strikes people like them not as a sign of the pastor's humility and informality, but as a mark of arrogance—you are unworthy of my preparation.

More troubling is the possible implication that God is unworthy of our preparation. I complain about the fastidiousness of my musicians, but I recall one of them, an organist, who—when I complained about the excessiveness of her rehearsal on the organ outside my study—replied, "After all, this is Bach; the music deserves it!"

The God who has graciously convened us deserves the best we have to offer. If it's worth doing for God, it's worth doing right.

Helena would want me to note a few things about this matter of giving our best:

1. Sunday worship is a visual affair. Matters like the posture of the leaders, visibility of their gestures, and the condition of vestments and paraments are important. Our attention to the visual details is an aspect of our service to the congregation, the liturgy that we do for God.

2. No one who is unprepared or to whom God has not given the gift of public reading of Scripture should read aloud in the Sunday assembly. There are folk in the congregation who have no other ministry than a good, clear, expressive voice for public reading.

Ask them to read on Sunday. God's Word is too important to be botched by poor reading. And, in the matter of public speaking or reading, what's good for the laity is essential for the clergy.

3. Music is a particular problem in many congregations because the teaching of choral and instrumental music is neglected, relegated to a "frill" in schools. Generally speaking, give us a well-played piano rather than an inadequate, poorly played electronic organ. Any style of music, contemporary or traditional, can be appropriate for Sunday worship if it meets theological criteria like, Who is the God being praised in the music? Is this music faithful to the witness of Scripture? Does this music enable the corporate worship of the church?

Music ought to be done well. If jazz or contemporary music is used, it ought to be played by those who play this music well. Otherwise, stick to the traditional. I believe the church may have to set aside more of its resources for the training of gifted, dedicated people who wish to be of service in the church's music ministry but who need more training.

Helena would also add white gloves for the acolytes, but I dare to think them optional. She would approve of the accolade given by a woman of my acquaintance to her young pastor: "Our pastor always leads us in worship as if something very important, something of life-changing significance were about to happen."

The other day, inspecting with an electrician the attic of Duke Chapel high above the sanctuary, I noted the wonderful workmanship of the fitted beams. Then, there, toward the base of one of these huge oak beams, carved into the wood where nobody but God could see it, I read, "John Scavonni, for the Glory of God."

Some unknown craftsman put a lifetime of skill into that beam that no one would ever see. Yet God sees. If it's worth doing for the glory of God, it's worth doing right.

Meaning the Music

Today, J. Benjamin Smith died of a dreaded disease that has taken a disproportionate number of his fellow organists and musicians. Ben was, for the past five years, not only my friend but also my musician.

The trouble between ministers and musicians is widely known. We are alleged to feel the same way about one another that cats feel about dogs. Ben was one of the most dear, most lively people I have ever known, although on occasion that did not keep me from wanting to strangle him to death with my bare hands.

One day, in one of our three-hour hymn selection marathons, Ben said to me, "You must realize that you are not a musician." To which I replied, "And I get down on my knees every night and thank God for it."

On the first Sunday in May, Mother's Day, as Ben and I were going into the sanctuary, he asked what the prospects were for a good sermon during the service. I replied, "Well, today's sermon is so weak that you should be prepared, after a cue from me, to stand and sing 'M Is for the Million Things She Gave Me.' It may be the only thing that will save us today."

One Christmas Eve at 10:30 P.M., just thirty minutes before the beginning of the service, everything came to a grinding halt when the guest boy soprano broke down in tears and refused to sing. "If my child does not want to sing," said his protective mother, "he does not have to sing."

"Let me have a chat with him," Ben said in a pleasant, soft voice. He took the sniffling boy in his office, shutting the door behind him. Once in the office, he grabbed the boy by his cassock and said, "Look, you little brat, you get out there and sing your heart out or I will twist your head off. You can't bully me! I've paid good money for that soprano to sing a duet with you and I don't intend to have it loused up by some spoiled brat. I've murdered tenors for less than this!"

Ben and the boy emerged from the office. "I think he's ready to sing now," said Ben in a reassuring voice. "The little man just needed it explained to him."

When Ben began to be sick, I started visiting him regularly. On one of those visits I asked him if he wanted to have prayer each time before I left. "No," he responded forthrightly. "Anything that I want to say to the Lord I have already said. I have always told

God everything that I had on my mind, even the inappropriate and socially unacceptable things. There's never been a problem between me and the Lord. So, when you come to visit me, don't bother with the prayer. Let's just talk about other people, laugh, and have a good time."

On my last visit with him, I told Ben everything I knew about everybody we knew—and it was wonderful.

After my five years of working with Ben, I came to a theory regarding the relations between ministers and musicians. I feel that a major cause of conflict between us is our different systems of value. As pastors, we are apt to cover over a multitude of sins, or at least incompetence, by an appeal to virtues like compassion, grace, and patience. "Aw, go ahead and let her sing the Mozart 'Alleluia' off-key," we say, "she means well." Thus we excuse incompetence, bad taste, poor preparation, or lack of talent within the church.

Musicians may be the last bastion of the notion that, if it's worth doing for God, it's worth doing right. Give of your best to the Master, and all that. It doesn't matter if the soprano is sincere, was good at it thirty years ago, has had a tough home life, or whatever; if she hasn't got it right, she hasn't got it right.

Sometimes the standards of musicians can lead them to perfectionism, conflict (especially with pastors without standards), and cantankerousness. But their presence is a constant reminder that God deserves our best efforts, that beauty is a goal worth giving one's whole life to achieve, and that God is greatly pleased by the creations of the disciplined human hand or voice.

When I began looking for a musician to replace Ben, a delegation of students from the chapel choir came to see me. They said that, while they knew there were lots of qualities that made for a good musician, they hoped that when I looked over the applicants I would look for someone with faith, the Christian faith. I asked them to say more and one of them, a freshman, said, "We want somebody who not only directs us toward beautiful religious music, somebody who not only sings it, but also means it. You could always tell that Ben really meant it."

I see no musical reason why a person could not sing the music of Bach or Bruckner beautifully, even if the singer did not believe the stuff of which the music sang. Yet something deep in me agrees with that freshman. All other things being equal, a musician ought to mean it in order to sing it.

One Sunday, while Ben was directing a piece with his usual flamboyance and exuberance—waving his arms in the air, body swirling, white surplice flapping wildly—a little girl in the first row was heard to say, "Look Mommy, he's trying to fly."

To my knowledge, Ben never was able to fly while he directed the chapel choir. But he certainly enabled us to soar, to break free of earth outrageously to sail into space on the wings of his beautiful, exuberant song.

Fearful, Wonderful Worship

In their insightful book *Rerouting the Protestant Mainstream*, C. Kirk Hadaway and David A. Roozen say that one of the most important things mainline Protestantism must do is to worship God. If we strike the world as nothing more than a sanctified form of Rotary, then we deserve the doom we shall get. Folk are hungry, say these two sociologists of religion, for a people who know mystery, who dare to explore the transcendent—people who risk worship of the living God.

I'm looking for that church. Are you?

Last year, on a bright summer Sunday, we worshiped with a little congregation in a fine old suburb of Berlin. The beautiful old church was only a few blocks from the Wannsee House where, just sixty years earlier, leaders of the Third Reich met and, over coffee and strudel, planned their "final solution" for exterminating all the Jews of Europe.

To our surprise, the small parking lot of the church was full, full of expensive cars. When we entered the church we could see why. There was to be a baptism. The proud parents, grandparents, and friends had gathered toward the front of the congregation, with the baby wrapped in elegant white linen and lace.

Here was "Cultural Christianity" at its best. I doubted if the family and friends had been in church often before that bright morning; perhaps they had been there on some Christmas past, or the last time they had celebrated a child born into the reigning culture.

The pastor stepped into the chancel, welcomed the congregation warmly, and prayed an opening prayer. At the conclusion of the prayer, as I had expected, there were three or four clicks and flashes of the assorted cameras, capturing everything for posterity. A gentle hum emanated from the amateur videographers.

"Excuse me," said the pastor, "this is not a press conference, a [now, in sarcastic English] 'photo opportunity'; this is God's church, this is a service of worship. When we are finished, you may take all of the photos you wish, but not now. This is what we call 'worship.' "

Everyone became very still.

Then we began to worship. After hymns, prayers, and Scripture, the pastor preached. He began his sermon by noting that parents today face heavy responsibilities. They must provide for the education, the safety, and the emotional well-being of their children. Children require resources, patience, and time.

"Unlike some previous generations," noted the pastor, "we have the opportunity to provide generously for the material needs of our children. We are able to buy them many things. . . ."

He continued, "Unfortunately, we are finding that it is much easier to give our children material gifts than to give them other gifts. Gifts like a reason for living, a purpose for life—where can these gifts be purchased in the stores?"

The congregation was still and attentive.

"These gifts, these gifts that matter, can only come as gifts from God. We have a word for it—grace. Therefore we pray that God will give our children what we can never give them—grace. We smother our children with gifts that corrupt, that deface and deform our children into superficial, materialistic adults because we are not good at giving, because we have not the resources to give them gifts that matter. Therefore we must pray to God to take our children, to give them gifts that matter. We offer our children back to the God who gave them to us, and dare to ask God to form them in God's image."

In a number of places the Bible claims that it is a fearful thing to be brought into the presence of the living God. A fearful thing. Yet on Sunday, in worship, even such fear can be life-giving. There, on a bright summer Sunday—in a church whose sad history is a grim memory of a time, just sixty years ago, when the church had not the resources to say no when *no* was needed—a courageous pastor enabled us to worship a free, living, demanding God.

That Sunday, we worshiped.

Quitting Time?

It was the last Sunday of the school year, and the phone was ringing at 8:00 in the morning. "Hello," I answered.

"Dr. Willimon, are you awake yet?" the undergraduate chapel attendant asked.

"Yes, of course I'm awake," I responded in an offended tone.

"Just wanted you to know there's no electricity in the chapel."

"What? No electricity? Is it dark?"

"Well, I had to get a flashlight in order to dial your number."

"That dark? Has the choir arrived yet?"

"I can hear people moving around down front, but I can't see anybody."

I rushed across town and arrived at a still totally dark chapel.

"Quick, go downstairs and get your hands on every candle we have—the used ones in the storage room, in the closet and everywhere," I told those milling about.

After a hectic forty-five minutes of scurrying around, we had about three hundred fifty candles lit, occupying every flat surface in the chapel. The candles only barely broke the darkness of the huge Gothic-style building. Having no electricity for the organ, we completely changed the service to accommodate a piano we pushed in from a nearby building. Fifteen minutes before the service was to begin, I was wringing wet with perspiration from shifting furniture and rewriting the service.

Then, in answer to someone's prayer—not mine at this point—
the electricity and all the lights snapped on. This meant that as the
majority of worshipers arrived they were greeted by a fully illuminated chapel filled with three hundred fifty burning candles.

"Well, well," said some smart-aleck sophomore as he entered
the chapel, "What has Dr. Willimon in store for us today?"

"Sit down and shut up" was my pastoral response.

Matters got worse. In all the confusion beforehand I had forgotten to put on my robe for the processional. The musicians were
confused, singing some hymns I thought we'd dropped, dropping
other hymns I thought we'd retained. Cues were missed—the
whole thing was a mess. I couldn't wait for the service to limp to
its sorry conclusion. Toward the end of the service, as I sat in my
seat, I thought, "There has got to be an easier way of making a living. This is ridiculous. God has no interest in a church at this location. I have to find some less stressful line of work."

Finally, I said the benediction, and the congregation filed out of
the chapel.

"I loved the candles," said one freshman. "Nice touch."

After everyone I could see had gone, three undergraduate
women approached me.

"Dr. Willimon, we are all seniors," one of them said. "We are
graduating next week. As we've thought about our time here at
the university, we consider Sundays in the chapel as among our
best memories of life here. We are going to miss these Sundays.
We wanted to thank you for enriching our lives and helping us
during our years here."

There was nothing I could say. Here I was all prepared to throw
in the towel and admit defeat, having convinced myself that
Christian ministry is completely futile, pointless and utterly ineffective. And here God sends these three wonderful people to tell
me their lives have been touched through this ministry.

Isn't that typical of God? Just when you get yourself all ready
to call it quits, God shows you it isn't over until God says it's
over. I don't know whether to be disgusted or grateful.

WILLIAM H. WILLIMON

Great Moments in Worship

I used to tell students that I was working on a book called *The Ten Worst Moments in the History of Liturgy,* or *Ten Worship Services Jesus Would Have Walked Out Of.* The students would bring me examples to consider for my Top Ten list. I noted that most of their nominations involved children's sermons — a liturgical practice not dear to my heart. (However, once when I wrote an article questioning the use of trite children's sermonettes, I received nearly as much negative mail as I did when I criticized racist Christian schools. So if you love to do children's sermons, please just do them well, and don't write me about it.)

After Easter one year a student told me this great story:

My field assignment is at this large church in a town near here. We have this young associate minister who is always trying something new. Well, on Holy Saturday I went by the church to check on a few things, and there was the associate, hard at work on something in the corner of the sanctuary. He was hammering away at what looked like a small stage set made out of plywood and papier-mâché. With fear and trembling, I asked him what he was doing.

"Have you ever read *The Velveteen Rabbit?*" he asked.

"Yes," I said. "It's a children's book, isn't it?"

"Right! Well, when it comes time for the children's moments tomorrow, I'm going to call the kids down front and read from *The Velveteen Rabbit.* I've got this stuffed rabbit here and I am going to stick it in this hole in my papier-mâché tomb, like this."

With that, he stuck the toy rabbit in the tomb.

"Then," he continued, "I'm going to count to three and pull out a live bunny rabbit from the tomb. Get it? Resurrection!"

"Does the pastor know that you are planning this?" I asked.

"No, not yet," he replied. "But won't he be surprised!"

"Yes, I daresay he'll be surprised — or something like that," I said. I stumbled out of the sanctuary, not knowing what to do. I decided to go over to the pastor's house, just across the yard. The pastor's wife met me at the door. Unfortunately, she said, her husband was out visiting a sick parishioner.

"I'm afraid that *he* will be ill after tomorrow's service," I said.

She asked me what was wrong, and I felt that I had to tell her. I described the tomb, the stuffed rabbit, and the live bunny. The pastor's wife stood there for a moment. Then she gritted her teeth and said: "Look, you go right back over there and tell that nincompoop that I am speaking for my husband when I say to get those damn rabbits—both stuffed and unstuffed—and that papier-mâché tomb out of the church, or *he* will have to be resurrected in order to serve a church ever again!"

Liturgical innovation postponed.

Getting Our Rites Right

With their extravagance, tasteless display, mix of the unashamedly pagan and the merely incipiently Christian, the saccharine solos and the crooning cousins, weddings are among the most distasteful of pastoral activities.

Though I have sometimes labored heroically to reform some of the weddings under my care, I have suffered silently through the recitations from Gibran, Buscaglia, and the Song of Songs, waiting for the day when some justice of the peace might assume responsibility for what has become essentially a secular affair.

I understand that in the early Middle Ages, in England, weddings were performed on the front porch of the church. As the church gained more political responsibility, weddings were moved inside. I would love to get them back on the front porch.

I recall the wedding I performed with George Baker. He is a retired Methodist preacher and Navy chaplain who does not suffer fools gladly. As George and I stood in the hallway waiting for the cue from the overbearing wedding director, I said, "I just don't feel good about this wedding. The groom is a jerk. He has been openly contemptuous of this whole enterprise. He sat through the premarital counseling with a smirk on his face. It all means nothing to him."

"Humph!" said George. "Then we must bear down on him."

"What?" I asked.

"Bear down on him. Put the fear of God in him! Make a believer out of the rascal!"

What George had in mind became clear to me only after we entered the sanctuary and the service had begun. George followed the same *United Methodist Book of Worship* I had in my hands. But not in the same way.

"Marriage is an honorable estate," George began solemnly. Looking intently and authoritatively into the eyes of the now-unnerved groom, he went on, "instituted by *Almighty God*."

The groom began to tremble slightly.

"It is not to be entered into *unadvisedly,*" George continued (now gripping the groom's hand), "but reverently, discreetly, and in the fear of God."

The groom began to whimper.

"I require and charge you both as you stand *in the presence of God*!" shouted George, seizing the groom by the lapel of his tux, "before whom the *secrets of all hearts are disclosed.*"

The groom was now weeping. The bride looked at me, utterly confused. When we finally moved closer to the altar, George and I helped the bride assist the groom up the steps. When it came time for him to respond to the vows, he spoke in a high, cracking voice, somewhat like that of a frightened child, or a young trapped squirrel.

George winked at me and patted the groom on the shoulder, saying, "There, there, son, it's going to be all right."

People can be changed, born again, done over, by participating in Christian ordinances. They effect that which they celebrate. George Baker taught me to expect the same of the service of holy matrimony.

The church can wring its hands over marriage ceremonies, lament the tasteless opulence of many weddings, accept the secular reality of most weddings, or it can try, like George, prophetically to create a new reality.

Section 4 | Congregational Life

The Church Is Not Our Cadillac

DURING HIS TENTH ANNIVERSARY SHOW, GARRISON Keillor told a story (he said it was true) about an experience he had as a teenager.

Walking down the sidewalk one day, he saw this unbelievably beautiful woman coming toward him. A stunningly beautiful woman. What could he do? He spied a large, white Cadillac parked next to the sidewalk. Strolling over to the Cadillac, he reached into his pocket, pulled out a dime, put it in the parking meter, and leaned confidently against the Cadillac, smiling at the approaching woman.

To his delight, she returned his smile. She moved toward him, spoke to him, saying "Thank you" as she got into the Cadillac and drove off.

Take this as a parable of ministry. The church is not our Cadillac. We pastors, leaders, teachers may be "stewards of the mysteries of God" (1 Cor. 4:1) but not owners. It is fine for us to make our contribution, to lean against the church in order to look good, but ultimately this Cadillac is God's and God has entrusted it to the *laos*, God's people rather than to the pastors of God's people.

Don't push this or any other homiletical metaphor too far. However, I think at least in a limited way it works.

Beginning in the 1900s, we North American Protestant clergy

have been under the grip of what many have called the "professional model of ministry." Emulating doctors and lawyers, we acted as if we had some sort of esoteric training or knowledge unavailable to others, as if our seminary training was the source of real ministry; as if we pastors were an upper crust of Christians from which ministry was meant to trickle down to the lowly laity.

This image has debilitated the pastoral ministry in our day, rendered the laity into passive spectators, and tempted us clergy to seek validation for our work in illegitimate places.

My last congregation had about six hundred members. I was the only "professional" (that is, full-time salaried) person on the church staff. With six hundred people to care for, a church to be administered, sermons to be prepared, plus a little writing, a little speaking on the side, there was no way that I could do it all. For the first time in my ministry I was forced, simply by the exigencies of the situation, to, at every turn in the road, ask myself, Can anyone in this church do this as well as I? I was amazed by how many tasks can be done as well by the laity as by the pastor.

Of course, when the pastor visits or teaches or administers, he or she will do so differently, his or her actions will be "read" differently than when performed by a layperson. However, the engagement of the laity is a visible reminder to both the world and to the pastor that the church's ministry is *the church's* ministry.

I went to a church trustee meeting when I arrived at Northside Church. At that meeting the trustees discussed problems with the church's roof and what to do about them. I made one comment in an hour of discussion and everyone looked at me like I was dumb. "We take it you don't know much about roofing," one trustee said.

That was the last trustee meeting I attended. Roofing, maintenance, facilities were their ministerial gifts, not mine. My absence from trustee meetings left me free to be present elsewhere.

Too often I have heard many laity complain that "Our pastor is not a spiritual leader." When I ask them what they mean, they usually say something like, "We asked for a morning Bible study, but he said he was too busy running the church gymnasium." Laity are justified in wondering what on earth we pastors are doing if we are too busy to lead Bible study, to plan worship, to pray. Not knowing exactly what to do as pastors, we will attempt to do everything out of fear that we might neglect doing those things that might justify our ministry. This is a way to clerical fatigue, bankruptcy of the spirit, not to mention a dead congregation that exists to be served rather than to serve.

Like any other pastor, I had a large number of persons in my congregation struggling with alcohol abuse problems. A couple of decades of experience with this particular pastoral care problem had convinced me that I wasn't very good with alcoholics. Calling together four or five recovering alcoholics in my congregation, I asked if they might be willing to serve as our congregation's ministers to this need. They all said yes. So whenever I encountered a family or a person struggling with alcohol, I would say, "Someone is going to call you this week about what you're going through. You may be surprised who calls you. I hope that you will be willing to let them help you, because this person knows, really knows, what you're going through. This person has a gift in this area."

Too often, if something needed doing in the church, I did it. If the youth needed leading, I led them. Then, when I left that congregation and moved on to another, people would say to me later, "You know, we had a great youth program when you were here. But after you left, it just died."

Dumb that I was, I took that as a compliment. Later I realized that was an insult rather than a compliment to my pastoral leadership. Pastors only have significance as the means through which God commandeers the people of God. We exist to "equip the saints," not to take their God-given ministry from them.

The church is not our Cadillac.

Divine Wisdom Among Little Old Ladies

A few years ago, a friend of mine returned from one of those National Council of Churches trips to the Soviet Union. Two weeks had made her a Soviet expert. When asked about the churches there, her reply was, "There's nobody left in the churches except for a few little old ladies."

Poor, out-of-it church. Nobody left but a few little old ladies.

In the light of more recent events, I think we are now better able to assess the relative importance of those few believing women. As it turned out, those women had put down their money on the right horse. While leaders of the National Council of Churches were busy having dialogue with the Communist bosses in Romania and elsewhere (the very same bosses who were making life so miserable for Christians there), the pastor of a little Romanian Reformed church, probably assisted by a few "little old ladies," was busy bringing down an empire. And as usual, no one was more surprised by all this than those of us in the church.

When will we ever learn the truth that God has chosen "what is foolish in the world to shame the wise; God chose what is weak in the world to shame the strong; God chose what is low and despised in the world, things that are not, to reduce to nothing things that are" (1 Cor. 1:27-28)? I know that this passage concludes with "so that no one might boast in the presence of God," but is it OK to boast in the presence of our half-hearted church that those believing women, that faithful pastor, knew a great deal more about the way the world works than all of the Pentagon strategists, White House-Kremlin planners, World Council of Churches dialoguers, and most of the rest of us?

At the World Methodist Conference one summer, my dean was talking with a bishop from one of the Baltic republics. "How in the world were you able to keep going with so many years of hostility and persecution?" he asked the bishop.

"Well, though it was tough, we in the church always took the long view," was his reply.

Back in the 1980s, the World Methodist Council gave Gorbachev its "Peacemaker of the Year" award. A couple of months later, he ordered the tanks into Lithuania. As far as I know, he did not return the award.

Is it possible for us to look behind the encouraging headlines coming out of the East, to take the long view, to read them sub specie aeternitatis, to let ourselves be schooled by those wise, so worldly wise, little old ladies who knew something that even the CIA did not?

I quickly learned, in my first parish, that if I really wanted something done, something pushy, a bit risky, something out of the ordinary, I needed to go to the members of the Alice Davis Memorial Circle of The United Methodist Women. It wasn't that they were all over seventy and had time, it was that they were all well formed as Christians and had faith. While Nixon was pondering whether to go to China, they were finishing the UMW Fall Mission Study on The People's Republic. When we all celebrated the end of the Vietnam War, they were sending letters to the people of Vietnam apologizing for our destruction of their country, putting aside a portion of their Social Security checks to contribute to the Church World Service refugee resettlement program. When I spoke to the church about the need to do something about the plight of the homeless, three of the women came forward to tell me that they work as volunteers at the homeless shelter, so, if I were really serious, they would be happy to take me for a visit.

Sometimes there is nobody left to be the church "except for a few little old ladies." Thank God.

Ambiguous Epiphany

Sometime ago, Morton Kelsey did a survey of mystical experiences and discovered, to the surprise of us rationalists, that a great majority of Americans report having had vivid, life-changing mystical visions. Divine appearances, epiphanies, theophanies, and other mystical experiences still happen to Americans. Or so they tell Kelsey.

Perhaps the most interesting fact about Kelsey's survey is that though most of these people say that their experiences are real and life-changing, they wouldn't dare tell their pastor because "he would think I was crazy." It's rather sad that the last person to whom most people would talk about seeing God is God's chief field representative. However, there are times when the less we pastors know about these epiphanies, the better.

Several years ago a woman ordered me to come to her house, where she told me: "I have called you over here because the most wonderful thing has happened. I have personally—right before my eyes, as big as life, just like you are sitting here—seen Jesus.

"About 2:00 or 3:00 in the morning I just sat straight up in bed," she explained. "I thought I heard someone call my name. At first I thought it might have been my indigestion. You know how bad the food at Leo's can be. But there, right at the foot of my bed, he was. As big as life. Actually, a little bigger than life. My Lord. He was dressed in white. Shining. Just like he is in the third window from the left on the right side of the church. And he called me by name.

"I said, 'Here I am, Lord,' or words to that effect. And he said, 'I want you to give your life to my work. I have work for you to do.' Then he was gone. That's why I've called you over here. I want to give my life totally, completely to the Lord and his work."

"Well," I said, "this is wonderful. Few of us receive such visions. And I am only too happy to help you think about what you can do to serve the Lord."

"That's what he said, 'Gladys, I have work for you to do.' "

"Well, let's see. Have you thought about teaching? The Fellowship Class lost a teacher last month. You might be just the one to—"

"Fellowship class!" she exclaimed. "Me teach the very people who were so haughty to me and Marvin when we first moved here? I would like to tell them a thing or two, but you don't want me to teach that crowd."

"Oh, I see. Well, how about the children's nursery? You know we have a real problem getting folks who can help keep the—"

"Preacher! Have you lost your mind? Can't you even remember visiting me in the hospital last year when my back went out? That would be suicide for me. Since when have you seen somebody able to look after little kids without being able to lift them?"

"That's true," I said. "You know, before you retired, you worked as a secretary, a typist. Now there's a job that needs doing at the church! If you would type for us a couple of mornings a week, we could—"

"Oh no, you don't," she said, "I thought I made myself clear when you went and bought that expensive typewriter that I was opposed to it. We had nothing but trouble with them in the office where I worked. But no, you thought you knew more about type-writers than anybody else, so you are stuck with it. Now nobody knows how to use it."

I made a couple more attempts to figure out what Jesus might have had in mind when he asked her to work for him, but to no avail. Finally I said: "Look, why don't you think about it? Perhaps you'll have another vision. And next time would you do me a favor? Don't let him get out of your bedroom without telling you *exactly* what he wants you to do."

Be Reconciled

When I was in graduate school, a fellow graduate student decided to measure preaching's effect upon the racial attitudes of a Southern congregation. He devised a questionnaire by which to measure the racial attitudes of people. He administered the questionnaire to his Georgia congregation. Then he preached a series of sermons in which he addressed some aspect of our racial dilemma from a biblical perspective. At the end of the series, he administered the questionnaire to those who had heard his sermons. Result: The congregation was 2.3 percent *more* racist after having heard the sermons than before!

When will we preachers learn? Rarely are people's deepest, most ingrained prejudices eradicated merely by telling them that they ought to change. The sources of our various prejudices lie deep, therefore their means of eradication must lie deep as well.

In my own denomination, we have worked at healing the sin of our racism. Alas, most of our work has been in the form of slo-gans, quadrennial programs, and top-down pronouncements. In the years that our Ethnic Minority Local Church Fund has been in effect, we have pumped millions into the effort. Disappointingly, the percentage of African American United Methodists has actu-ally declined during the same period. We have a large percentage of African American bishops, a number of general church agency heads who are African American, but little change at the grass roots in the local congregations, in the individual hearts and minds of our members. Top-down pronouncements, racial quotas, subsidies, and slogans do not make for reconciliation.

Racism—our long, sad history of dealings with one another in black and white—is deeper, more perplexing, impervious to merely educational, or even homiletical, remedies. There may be evils that can be eradicated through government programs, sloganeering, the collection and dissemination of more data. But this is the sort of demon that can be driven out only through prayer (Mark 9:29). We are not contending against flesh and blood (Eph. 6:12), that which may be modified through a few better laws, more rigidly enforced quotas, a token bishop or two. We are fighting with the powers, with principalities, rulers of the present darkness, the demon lurking within our own hearts.

Our Christian fight with the evil of racism, our continuing effort as Christians to do right in black and white and other shades as well, founders amid our sincere but still superficial efforts. Wherein is our hope?

My friend Robert Howell, Jr., a pastor in South Carolina, has told me of a program that is making a difference in his church, "Promise Keepers." Here, evangelical men confront their sin of racism. Howell says, "Evangelical men have historically carried their prejudices in one hand and their Bible in another. Through 'Promise Keepers,' they are beginning to gain the spiritual resources to admit that they can no longer do that and be Christian."

After decades of frustration in his work in a mainline denomination to minister to the sin of racism, Howell claims that at last, "I'm having historically racist people from the South who are coming to me and saying, 'We must do something *as Christians* about the scandal of our racism.' 'Promise Keepers' recruits a group of church men who will get up for an interracial breakfast at 6:00 A.M. and participate in an eight-week course with follow-up sessions. The course takes the form of a spiritual pilgrimage, beginning with Bible study and prayer, continuing to that point where you learn to hold one another accountable for your Christian walk, particularly your walk toward racial reconciliation."

During this pilgrimage, Christian men, black and white, enter into dialogue with one another, dialogue buttressed by intense prayer and soul-searching. White males are led to confess their complicity—active and passive complicity—in the continuing structures of racism. They are then brought to a face-to-face confrontation with African American males in which they apologize to them for participating in racial bigotry. "Promise Keepers" believes that the Christian faith has the resources to move men to confession, believes that we will never get beyond our racism until we first confess our sin, face-to-face, to one another. A first step comes in the bold ownership of our sin, in honest admission that we have participated in and profited from the unjust structures and attitudes of racism. "Promise Keepers" believes that such risky confession, such costly discipleship can come only from a deep, honest, and engaging experience of the love of God in Jesus Christ.

Howell recalls the man who came to him and, with tears in his eyes, said, "They want me to do something I don't want to do. They want me to stand next to a black man, embrace him, and tell him I've sinned, tell him I'm sorry. I'm not sure I'm sorry."

Howell counseled the struggling man, "Don't just do this for the other man, do it for *you*. Become what God intends for you to be." The man took the bold step and was reconciled.

The Christian faith claims that an encounter with the risen Christ enables birth, new life, and conversion. *Metanoia*. We in the church ought to demonstrate the truth of that claim not just by preaching about racial reconciliation, but by producing the sort of disciples who embody that claim in their own lives.

A Child's Sermon

It was a cold Christmas Eve a few years ago and my family was running late for the communion service. Where are my sermon notes? Who has my collar? Don't forget to turn off the lights. Everybody in the car and keep quiet.

On the way to church, my five-year-old daughter, who had

been looking rather pale all day, finally got sick, throwing up in the car. "Great," I thought. "if people only knew what preachers go through."

I wheeled into the church parking lot and jumped out, leaving my wife, Patsy, to clean up the car and get the kids into church. If people only knew what preachers' spouses go through.

Patsy led a still unsteady and pale Harriet into the church, suggesting that they sit on the back pew, in the darkness, in case she got sick again. Our son William, age seven, ran down to the front of the church to join his visiting grandparents.

I hastily threw on my robe, took a deep breath, and joined the choir for the processional. I made it through the first part of the service, and the sermon. Then came the Eucharist. I prayed, broke the bread, poured the wine, and invited everyone forward for communion.

Patsy said it never occurred to her to suggest that Harriet go forward to receive communion. After all, she wasn't feeling well, despite it being the night before Christmas. Patsy went down, then returned to her seat in the darkened rear of the church. She noticed William get up from where he was sitting and go back to the communion rail. What was he up to? She watched him race to the back of the church and scoot down the pew toward his sister.

He opened his hands, revealing a small piece of bread. "Harriet, the body of Christ, given for you."

Without hesitating, she picked the bread out of his hands and plopped it into her mouth, saying, "Amen."

William slid back down the pew and ran to join his grandparents.

I don't mean to be sentimental, and I hate it when we preachers tell cute stories about our kids, but I want to ponder the significance of the fact that, when God chose to come among us, God chose to come as a child.

As a big, grown-up, responsible adult, I am quite adept at making myself the center of the world, turning even religion into something that revolves around me and my big, adult responsibilities. I get so consumed by the necessary, the required, the expected, and the accustomed that sometimes I forget to pay attention. So God sends a child as a harbinger ("this shall be a sign unto you"), like a road sign pointing the way, or a stop sign to stop us dead in our tracks, someone to get our attention.

One day Jesus was walking with his disciples, teaching them. All were taking notes, trying hard to pay attention. They said to Jesus, "Can't something be done about these children? Send them to children's church or the nursery or something. They are distracting."

And do you remember what Jesus did? He said, "When you receive one such child [surprise!] you receive me."

The child is here to distract us from our big, serious, but utterly self-centered adult religion, in order that baby Jesus might get our attention and lead us toward a kingdom that, according to him, has a very small door through which only the small can enter.

Pat and Me

Would the person who introduced me to Pat Robertson please identify yourself? Without you, I would have never met the man, would have never known a real-live presidential candidate, would have never received these monthly mailings, these evening telephone calls for money. Without you, Pat would have never known me. With friends like you, I don't need enemies.

My relationship with Pat Robertson began this fall when I received a packet of tapes and pamphlets proclaiming that I had just joined Pat's *700 Club*. My letter, personally signed by Pat, told me that, because of my generous support, I was reaching millions of people every day through *The 700 Club*. I also kept a telephone line open so that thousands of prayer requests could get through (4 million called last year); clothed, fed, and met the needs of millions of people through Operation Blessing; sustained CBN University; and helped "to restore a biblical consensus to America." I would have felt great except that I had not given a dime to Pat. Someone else deserves the credit. Would you please identify yourself?

I really felt guilty when I received a gold *700 Club* pin, a membership card, a copy of the CBN Partnership newsletter, two cassette tapes on "Pat Robertson's Four Principles of Success," as well as my first Monthly Giving Card telling me that my gift would be used in accordance with Ezra 7:17-18. A check of Ezra 7:17-18 indicates that Pat plans to use my generous contribution to purchase "bulls, rams, and lambs." Don't they have livestock ordinances in Virginia Beach? No wonder the *700 Club* reaches millions. You can smell it all the way to Richmond! If Pat was able to reach millions through the use of bulls, rams, and lambs, that's fine. But Ezra 7:18 troubled me because it tells Pat, "Whatever seems good to you and your [brethren] to do with the rest of the silver and gold, you may do . . ." (RSV).

I wrote and told Pat that, while I would love to take the credit for keeping his university afloat, the telephone lines open, Operation Blessing blessing, a biblical consensus restored, and bulls, rams, and lambs off the street, someone else had given the money in my name. I said if he would be kind enough to tell me who sent the money for me, I would like to have prayer with this person.

In answer to my letter I received my December *700 Club* Monthly Giving Card asking for a gift of $15 or more to share the gift of eternal life.

One of these CBN newsletters had an awfully interesting story about a woman who does diets for the Lord—Born Again Body, Inc. There was also a piece about a Christian chef who whipped up a raspberry milkshake in a chocolate bag, and a story about Phil and Louis Palermo, who were going to demonstrate their spaghetti-throwing act that month on the *700 Club*. We members were also informed that Pat had designated his son, Tim, to be CBN's new president. I wrote Pat and asked why we members didn't get a chance to vote on Tim. In response, Pat sent my Monthly Giving Card for March asking for a sacrificial contribution to support the work. I felt better about Tim when I learned, in the CBN Partnership Newsletter, how the Lord had once led Tim to give $1,000 to CBN just before he was to get married, money Tim had been saving for a honeymoon. The next day, a man walked up and offered to send Tim and his new bride anywhere in the world. Tim and Lisa honeymooned in Greece. How would I have learned all of this without knowing Pat?

Where do I go to thank the person who joined me to the *700 Club* and introduced me to Pat? To whom do I owe gratitude for the monthly mailings as well as the periodic telephone calls from someone in Virginia Beach named Gladys asking me for money?

When I received my first personal correspondence from Pat, I thought not of rams and bulls in Ezra 7, but of the farmer that Jesus tells about in Matthew 13:24-30. Upon learning of the anonymous "gift" of some weeds amidst his grain, the farmer spoke for me, as well as for Pat, when he observed, "An enemy has done this."

Whoever you are, wherever you are, know this: With friends like you, Pat and I don't need enemies.

Keeping Work in Its Place

George MacLeod, founder of the Iona Community of Scotland, said that he took the job of cleaning the community's toilets so he would "not be tempted to preach irrelevant sermons on 'the dignity of all labor.' "

I haven't preached many sermons on the subject of work. Maybe I ought to. When I do preach on work, I will tell the congregation that I believe the fabled "Protestant work ethic" is a decidedly mixed inheritance for the church. Martin Luther attacked medieval monasticism by dignifying all work as divinely ordained. You don't have to become a nun to serve God. Even the lowest servant cleaning floors in the rich man's house mops to the glory of God. God did not simply create the world and quit. God keeps creating and invites us, in even the humblest work, to join in God's continuing creativity.

Luther's thought on work is not so much a glorification of our human work, but rather a celebration of the work of God. When Luther uses *vocation,* he uses it more to refer to tasks like marriage and family than to jobs. Our vocation is not work but *worship*.

Sometime ago I saw a book for Christian students. It began: "How can you serve Christ on campus?" Answer: "First by studying hard. You are called to be a student. You have gifts and graces from God for study. You are not studying just for yourself, but for what you can eventually give to others through your study. Now, study!"

That sounds like "vocation."

Unfortunately the "Protestant work ethic" tended to elevate even the meanest, most miserable job to the status of divinely ordained, so that today when we say "vocation," we mostly mean "job." And that's not right.

Sometimes the Protestant work ethic defended the indefensible. If you're in a demeaning, degrading job, it is because God put you there; therefore, don't strive to better your condition. Such thought was a powerful hindrance to revolutionary thought and action.

Today, most people can expect *seven* job changes in their lifetime. Many of these will be forced upon people by external economic factors. How can these multiple changes, forced upon the worker by the system rather than by God, be called aspects of divine vocation?

While Protestantism, in its attempt to honor all work as a vocation from God, may have contributed to some of the abuses of capitalism, the Christian and the Jewish faiths also bear within a prophetic critique of work. In Genesis, humanity is graciously invited by God to work. God creates a garden, then invites the woman and the man to tend the garden. Yet Genesis also admits that work, a gracious gift of God, can also be a curse, when abused and used in sinful ways. Adam and Eve are cursed with hard work when they're kicked out of God's garden.

We have no record that Jesus ever worked or urged anyone else to do so. The "call" of Jesus appears to be a call to ordinary people like fishermen and tax collectors to leave their careers and to follow him on his travels about Galilee.

Thus, while work may be a good gift of God, our present structures of work are not divinely ordained. Work, like any human endeavor—sex, money, art—may be tainted with human sin. For some, that sin will take the form of *idolatry,* in which we give to our jobs honor and energy that should be reserved for God.

I think that we pastors ought to be cautious about claiming too much for work. Most of work's rewards are most mundane. For one thing, most of our friendships are somehow related to our work. One of the most dehumanizing aspects of unemployment is the loneliness of the unemployed. Also, from a Christian perspective, your work has value because it contributes not to your well-being, but to someone else's. As a mechanic said to me recently, "People need me more than they need a brain surgeon. [Some days, in Durham, it does seem as if we have more brain surgeons than auto mechanics.] When I put somebody's car back on the road, they're grateful and I'm happy." Work is a major way we discover our dependency on one another, our connectedness in a wide web of other persons' work.

For another thing, most of us work for the mundane, but utterly necessary, need to earn a living. Our work puts bread on the table. Rather than debate which forms of work contribute to our personhood and which do not, we ought to focus on which work fairly compensates a worker and which work doesn't. We ought to admit that most of us work for pay. While we are working for pay, we can achieve many other noble human values. But none of those noble values should deter us from the most basic value, that all ought to have work and that all ought to be justly compensated for their work. A fair, living wage is more to the point than our high-sounding theological platitudes.

We are right to seek meaningful work, since work is a major task given by God to humanity. We are right to criticize our present structures of work, expecting them to be sinful and in need of reform in various ways. Our work, suggests our faith, is a source of great joy, also of much pain. Making a life is more significant than making a living.

Ministry to Those *Not* in Crisis

The gospel is addressed to those *in extremis*. At the point of our greatest need, in the midst of our deepest crises, Christ reaches out to us. Those of us who are pastors know how to bring a comforting word, a healing touch to people in crises.

Few of us, thank God, live our lives in perpetual crises. We have our good days and, for most of us, the good days outweigh the bad, thank God. We have our moments when the world appears to shift under our feet and things fall apart and we are cast down. Yet most of the time the sun shines, and we are content and at peace.

What is the gospel word then?

I remember hearing the great George Buttrick speak, shortly before he died, saying to us gathered pastors, "Most any pastor can be helpful to people in time of need. It doesn't take a skillful pastor to visit someone in the hospital and be helpful. When people are sick, they are desperate, grateful for any word, even an inadequate word. Even an inept pastor will be well received in a family where the breadwinner has just been laid off from his job, where the mother has just learned that she has cancer, where the troubled teenager has just run afoul of the law."

Buttrick continued, "Such moments, when people are down and desperate, are not really the greatest tests of our ministry. The greatest tests are those moments when people are not down, not desperate, not at the end of their rope. There is where they often find out just how faithful our gospel really is. In those moments the pastor has the opportunity to become a prophet, to speak a word not merely of comfort, but of truth. And where is the pastor at those moments?

"So it takes a real pastor," Buttrick continued, "to go into a family where someone has just been promoted to presidency of the local bank and say, 'Mary, I've just gotten the news of your promotion. So I rushed right over knowing that this promotion is placing you in an extremely vulnerable position, as far as your soul is concerned. I wanted to come over and stand beside you during this time of potential temptation. Could we pray?'"

I remember discussing a fellow pastor with a friend. "Joe is really a wonderful pastor," I said. "Every time I go to the hospital, Joe is there. I am utterly amazed by how much he can be available to his people and their needs."

My friend replied, "Joe does most of that for Joe."

I thought this a rather severe judgment. My friend continued,

"By constantly enmeshing himself in other people's needs, by lurching constantly from crisis to crisis, Joe is preserved from ever having to reflect upon the value of what he is doing. There is a style of ministry, which I fear Joe embodies, of ambulance chasing, of becoming so engulfed in the crises of others, that he never has to ask tough questions of himself and the ultimate value of his ministry."

Most any of us can be helpful to people when they find out that their cherished daughter has not been admitted to the college of her choice. But it takes great pastoral fortitude to be present with a family when their son has just received his acceptance to Harvard. It takes a real prophet to help people see how we are, spiritually speaking, most vulnerable and at risk in moments of success, power, and health.

Most of us as pastors spend much of our time with people who are relatively content, relatively happy, and more or less at ease. These people, and their contentment, may be our greatest pastoral challenge.

The Visit

I knocked at the door of the little house. It was my second week in this parish, my second week of working through the congregants' homes. I had dressed casually to help people feel at ease. Sarah Jones was visit number 18. "Mrs. Jones?" I asked the small figure that peered at me through the shaded screen door.

"Yes, come in!" she said in a jovial tone. "I've been hoping you might come by this week. I'm thrilled to see you."

Although I was surprised that she'd been waiting for me, I was pleased that she was glad I'd finally come. After I sat down on her rose-colored couch, she asked, "Now that you're at last here [*"At last"? I'd been in town only two weeks!*] what do you need from me?"

"Need? Well, nothing really. I first wanted to get to know you better," I said. She seemed annoyed by this. Perhaps she was the shy type. I would have to draw her out.

"Let's begin by you telling me something about your family," I said. "How long have you been a widow?"

"Ten years," she said wistfully. "Paul died ten years ago last month."

"I'm sorry. How did he die?"

"Well," she said with some obvious discomfort, "he took his own life."

"I'm sorry," I said again. "And your children?"

I heard about Paul Jr.'s job in Seattle, about Sarah Lea's work as an attorney. She told me she had two grandchildren. When told about Sarah Lea's divorce, I asked Sarah to describe how she felt about that. We explored her ambivalence toward her son-in-law, his infidelities and sexual indiscretions. When told that Sarah Lea's marriage was "doomed from the beginning," I asked what Sarah meant by that. As it turns out, Sarah Lea was pregnant before her marriage and felt forced to marry; even though she secretly despised her husband.

From here our conversation turned back to Sarah's own marriage. I asked her about her negative feelings about her husband's death. When she said she "couldn't help feeling guilty," I asked her to elaborate. She was reluctant, but with some additional encouragement she discussed her feelings, occasionally wiping tears from her eyes. "But why must we talk about such things?" Sarah finally asked. "This is all very painful for me."

"Because I want to know as much about you as possible," I said. "We're beginning a relationship with each other. How can I truly help you if I don't know you, *really* know you?"

"Well, yes," she said. "I'm sure I'll enjoy knowing you, but all this is considerably more than I expected."

"What did you expect?" I asked.

"Well, this is all very new for me," she said in a halting voice, her lips trembling. "Paul always handled this sort of thing. I suppose I never realized how much was involved. I thought it was only a matter of you coming by here, assessing the situation and then giving me some estimate of cost. Then, you know, getting down to work."

"Giving you some estimate? What do you need?" I asked in

perplexity. "I don't know what you need until we talk, until you tell me."

"But that's *your* job, not mine," she said with some indignation. "Look around. Isn't it obvious to you?"

Then with a look of suddenly dawning, shocked recognition, she said, "Wait a minute. You're the new preacher! I thought you were the housepainter. I've been waiting all week for the man to give me an estimate on painting the house. I get it, you're the preacher, not the painter!"

Pastoral Conversation

"I believe that my latest bout began when my neighbor installed this mercury vapor light in her backyard. I don't have to tell you what those things do to a person! I tell you, my valic waves were out of sync something terrible! Couldn't sleep at night. And what it did to my refrigerator! Are you with me?"

I'm trying real hard to follow.

"And don't tell me that Phil Donahue is not to blame! I watch him every morning. And what does he know? Don't you defend Sally Jessy Raphael to me, either!"

I wouldn't think of it.

"Good. Recycling is the only answer. Every aluminum can we save helps to restore the balance. Although glass, especially green glass, well, of course that's an entirely different matter."

You're losing me again.

"Preacher, pay attention. What do they teach people in seminary these days? Well, it's been a long time since you were in seminary. I can't blame you. You have so many demands made upon you, what with your hobbies and all. But you really have got to investigate the seriousness of mercury vapor lights. I think my neighbor is trying to torture me to death with hers. I can tell what it's doing to the bugs. And if the Russians ever get them, what are we to do?"

Russians?

"I know that you hate George Bush."

What?

"Don't lie to me! You may have everyone else fooled, but not me. I can figure out your politics just by listening to your sermons. Like I said, I know that you hate George Bush, but I feel as if I understand him. I feel as if I'm the only person in the world who could really help him."

In what way could you help him?

"Well it's obvious, isn't it? Like Mr. Bush, I am sexualphobic myself."

What? Sexualphobic?

"Don't act so surprised. Everybody knows it about Mr. Bush, but not everybody knows it about me. It's true, I admit it. I wrote Mr. Gorby and told him about Mr. Bush's problem. I thought it might help him, when he was negotiating for wheat and computers, to know the sort of man he was dealing with. If only Mr. Bush would reach out and ask for help, talk things over with someone who could understand. Does he have a pastor? Well, being sexualphobic and all, what good could a pastor do him? Right?"

Right.

"And Mr. Gorby's wife's hats! What can I say?"

What, indeed?

"And another thing. What have you got against reincarnation? You're so big on ecology. Did it ever occur to you that people might treat their garbage a little differently if they knew that someday they might come back as a bug in a solid waste dump?"

I never thought of that.

"I'm not surprised. You have such a limited worldview."

Yes, yes I do. I'm realizing that I am limited.

"Limited and sheltered. Did I ever tell you that I once had an affair with James Brown's trumpet player?"

No. I don't think that you ever mentioned that to me.

"You probably forgot."

I don't think I would forget something like that.

"Well, I did have an affair. I was all dressed in red then—and you can only imagine why! And I was wearing this wet, white turban on my head twenty-four hours a day to keep in my theric forces, of course. As it turns out, we had known each other in a former existence and he recognized me. Although I didn't recognize him, at least not in his human form. But who could blame me for that? My astral body was totally out of control then, similar to yours right now. And I couldn't be blamed for the dumb things I did or said. You know what I mean."

I do?

"I worry about you sometimes, preacher."

You? You worry about me?

"Well, here you sit. Nothing to do. Surrounded by mercury vapor lights, wires within computers. I worry about your theric forces. No turban. No hat! But then, look at poor Mr. Bush. It makes me wonder what you might have been in a previous existence. Sometimes it's just too much to think about."

Life is complicated, isn't it?

"Oh, don't put that in a sermon! That's not a very profound thought, I must say. But then again, I have no idea which body you may be in right now. Did I tell you I once had an affair with James Brown's trumpet player?"

I believe you did.

Ministrations

I have sometimes bragged that I am an excellent church administrator, principally because I so dislike administration. When I came to my present job, for the first time in my ministry I had major administrative responsibilities. A big budget to oversee, two dozen employees—I was nervous. So I read Thomas Peters and Robert H. Waterman, Jr.'s then best-selling book on management, *In Search of Excellence* (Warner, 1988).

About the only thought I retained from *In Search of Excellence* was Peters' observation that most decisions do not improve with age. If you have a tough decision to make or some onerous job to do, then do it first thing in the morning. Stewing about it, dreading having to tackle it, will only make matters worse. Generally speaking, your first impulse to act on something will not change by putting the action off to a later date. So go ahead and do it now.

What this insight meant for me in my new job was that I tried to perform all of my administrative tasks early in the day, first thing in the morning, so that I could have the rest of the day for more specifically ministerial, priestly tasks. I think I'm a good church administrator because I discipline myself to devote so little time and energy to administration.

I worry about fellow pastors who proudly assert that they spend much of their day carefully administering the church. Not that administrative tasks are unimportant. It's simply that most of our administrative duties—answering mail, telephoning, preparing Sunday's bulletin, calling meetings, attending meetings—are not what makes us pastors and priests who we are for the church.

I agree with Henri Nouwen when he says, "If pastors don't know what is absolutely essential for them to do, then they will do the merely important."

The philosopher Alasdair MacIntyre says that we are increasingly in the grip of bureaucratic rules administered by the real high priests of our culture—the "managers," those persons without feeling, insight, or principles who simply write rules and apply them, managing conflicting claims without making a judgment, working with no goal or vision in mind other than management. Pastors are not called to manage but to lead. If we allow the managerial aspects of the pastoral ministry to crowd out energies devoted to the more visionary and priestly functions of ministry, then the church suffers.

I recall the layperson who, with great contempt, spoke of his pastor's boast that, "We have the best pastoral care delivery system in this town."

"Picture yourself in the hospital, dying of cancer," said the layperson. "Your pastor comes in, pats you on the shoulder, has a prayer, and leaves. You have just been the beneficiary of 'the best pastoral care delivery system in this town.'"

E. Brooks Holifield, in his wonderful book *A History of Pastoral Care in America* (Abingdon, 1983), has documented how we pastors have, time and again in our history, chameleon-like taken on the coloring of our surrounding culture, fashioning ourselves on the basis of whatever image of success and power the culture offered. The image of the busy pastor, schedule book in one hand and briefcase in the other, hurrying to the next meeting, is not a particularly inspiring image for our time.

I'll admit it, I'm a United Methodist. I can't speak for the sins and temptations of other ecclesiastical families, but in my United Methodist family, one of our greatest ministerial distractions is administration. We have a rule and two committees for everything. If a United Methodist minister doesn't want to be a priest, he or she can always go to a meeting. This is a big problem for us. When asked, "What do you think our bishops could do to change our church for the better?" I once replied, "The best thing our bishops could do is to declare a moratorium on meetings for one year. If our bishops would not go to any meetings and would just pray, read the Bible, teach and preach for a year, I think it would make a great deal of difference." I really mean that.

When I was a young pastor at my first appointment in rural Georgia, I was befriended by the pastor at the large, successful church at the nearby county-seat town. In the fall, we had our district meeting where all of us pastors were to appear before the district superintendent and render our twenty pages of annual reports.

I wanted to do well in my first ministerial appointment. So I stayed up half the night before the meeting, carefully typing out all of my reports, double-checking all of the attendance and giving figures ("Was that twenty people in attendance on July 7, or was that twenty-two?"). My reports bound in a plastic cover, typed to perfection, I proudly bore them to the meeting.

When I arrived at the parsonage of my senior colleague, he asked me to drive us in his black Buick to the meeting. "I didn't get much sleep last night as I was down at the jail with one of our teenagers who went astray. Took me until 2:00 A.M. to get him out."

As I guided his car through the Georgia countryside on the way to the meeting, he asked me, "Have you got a pen?"

"A pen?" I asked. I fumbled in my coat pockets, but all I could find was a pencil.

"That'll do. Give it to me," he said. Then, on his knee, as I drove, he began hastily filling in numbers and names on various sheets of paper. I looked out of the corner of my eye and saw that he was filling out his annual reports. In pencil! In a Buick!

At the meeting, I presented my reports, bound in the blue plastic folder, typed. He presented his reports, in fisted wad, in pencil.

To my knowledge, neither of us ever heard from our district superintendent regarding those reports. To my knowledge, neither of our congregations was any better, though certainly no worse, for the administrative effort, or lack of it.

I learned that day: In matters of church administration, it pays to distinguish the utterly essential from the merely important.

Do You Know Where Your Children Are?

"There's a man calling who is really upset," my secretary said.

"I figured as much," I said. "Was it my sermon comparing George Bush to King Eglon the Fat, or the one in which I argued that Shirley MacLaine resembles the Witch of Endor?"

"No, we still haven't had any responses to any of your sermons," the secretary responded. "This man's mad over something you have done to his daughter."

"What? Put him on and don't eavesdrop," I said.

"I hold you personally responsible," he began in a most exasperated and agitated tone.

"For what?" I asked.

"My daughter. We sent her there to get a good education. She is supposed to go to medical school. She is to be a third-generation nephrologist. Now she has got some fool idea in her head about Haiti, and I hold you personally responsible," he said.

"Please," I said, "could we try to be rational?"

He told me who he was, who his daughter was. I knew her, but not that well. She ushered nearly every Sunday in the chapel. She had also been active in various campus causes and had been one of the organizers of the spring Mission Workteam the year before. How could anybody be upset about a daughter like her?

"Like I said," he said, "she was supposed to go to medical school. Her grades are good enough. Now this."

"Now what?" I asked.

"Don't act dumb, even if you are a preacher!" he shouted into the telephone. "You know very well. Now she has this fool idea about going to Haiti for three years with that church mission program and teaching kids there. She's supposed to be a nephrologist, not a missionary for heaven's sake!"

"No pun intended," I said.

"None of this would have happened if it had not been for you. She has become attached to you, liked your sermons. You have taken advantage of her when she was at an impressionable age. That's how she got so worked up over this fool idea about going to be a missionary."

"Now just a minute. Didn't you take her to be baptized?" I asked.

"Well, yes, but we are Presbyterians," he said.

"And didn't you take her to Sunday school when she was little? You can't deny that. She told me herself that you used to take her to Sunday school," I said triumphantly.

"Sure we did. But we never intended for it to do any damage," he said.

"Well, there you have it," I said. "She was messed up before we ever got her. Baptized, Sunday-schooled, called. Don't blame this thing on me. *You* were the one who started it. You should have thought about what you were doing when you had her baptized."

"But we are only Presbyterians," he said, his once belligerent voice changing to a whimper.

"Doesn't make any difference. The damage was done before she ever set foot in our chapel. Congratulations, Mr. Jones, you just helped God make a missionary."

"We just wanted for her to be a good person. We never wanted anything like this."

"Sorry. You're really talking to the wrong person," I said, trying to be as patient as possible. "We only work with what we get. If you want to complain, you'll have to find her third-grade Sunday school teacher. The thing is quite out of our hands. Have a nice day."

It's eleven o'clock on Sunday morning. Do you know where your children are?

WILLIAM H. WILLIMON

The Reverend Grandma

According to Carlyle Marney, "God will use any handle to get hold of somebody."

Divine persistence and resourcefulness are, according to Scripture, virtually without limits. Bessie Parker was the handle God used to take hold of South Carolina for more than three decades until her death a few years ago. Bessie, who became a pastor in 1950, wore out automobiles the way her Methodist circuit-riding ancestors went through horses, routinely driving 30,000 miles every year. Although she had a reputation for being one of the most effective preachers in the South Carolina Conference of The United Methodist Church, she was the bane of the bishops. Churches complained when they heard that they were getting a "lady preacher"—and they resisted even more obstinately four years later when the bishop dared to move "our dear Reverend Parker" somewhere else.

With snow-white hair and a soothing southern drawl, she epitomized everyone's stereotype of a grandmother. This she used for everything it was worth. Preachers stood in line to enlist Bessie to lead their annual mission-fund appeals. When she got to preaching, telling congregants how much they were going to enjoy sending breeder pigs down to Haiti ("They will go on there and make more piggies in the name of the Lord," Bessie would giggle), pigs started packing. When one church repeatedly refused to fix its leaking church roof, the members were scandalized one Monday morning by the sight of their pastor—white hair, blue jeans and all—atop the roof, hammering away. The roof was quickly repaired with everyone's willing assistance. "It just don't look right to have your grandmother up fixing the roof," one church officer commented.

Toward the end of Bessie's ministry, the bishop sent Bessie to a very difficult church, one infamous for feuding, contentiousness, racism, and animosity toward the denomination. Before Bessie arrived, the church had run off two preachers in six months. Members had consistently refused to send any money to support denominational programs. The bishop seemed cruel to send Bessie there just before her retirement. Everyone predicted disaster.

A few months passed without my hearing a word about Bessie. Then I saw her at a denominational meeting and, fearing the worst, asked her how she was getting along at her new appointment.

"The sweetest people I have ever known!" she exclaimed. "Our first work team will leave for Brazil next month. I've got to get back early; this is our music weekend with the neighboring African American congregation."

I was dumbfounded. Were we talking about the same church? What about its hatefulness? Its racism? Had there been no problems?

"Not really," replied Bessie. "There was one little misunderstanding when we voted on this year's budget."

"Misunderstanding?"

"Yes. We got to the apportionment for the Black College Fund. When we were about to vote on acceptance, the chairman of our board said, 'Reverend Parker, we don't give no money to that because we ain't paying for no niggers to go to college.'"

"Oh no! What did you do?" I asked.

"I stood up and said, 'John, that's not nice. You sit down and act like a Christian.' Everything else passed without a single problem."

Who's going to misbehave in front of his grandmother?

Richard Baxter advised seventeenth-century Protestant pastors that "the tenderest love of a mother should not surpass ours" for our people. Bessie routinely mothered the people toward the Kingdom, using any handle she could to get across the gospel — just as God used Bessie. Thank God.

Section 5 | Evangelism

Going Public with the Peculiar

FOR SOME REASON THEOLOGIANS AT THE UNIVERsity of Chicago tend to talk much about "public theology," though I have yet to meet any people on the street in Chicago who have ever heard of David Tracy or Martin Marty. Still, I am all for going public with the gospel, letting our light shine, as someone has put it. It is of the very nature of the gospel to be public, to be witnesses "to Jerusalem, and Judea, . . . and to the end of the earth" (Acts 1:8 RSV). From what I know of church history, the problem is not whether or not we will go public, but how. What truth will be illuminated when our light shines? To which god will we witness when we go public?

Any theology worth bothering the public with begins in confrontation with the peculiar story called the Bible. Sometimes advocates of public theology act as if that story is a hindrance to rather than the occasion for Christians going public. They want the peculiarities of the story adjusted to suit the limitations of the public. Give the public credit, I say; there are good reasons, reasons having to do with the peculiarity of the gospel itself, for not listening to or believing in the gospel.

At what points the church's peculiar message leads to rejection by our non-believing neighbors depends, of course, upon the neighbors. However, we have no way of removing the basic political challenge posed by the gospel to all counterpolitical schemes.

I'm all for political responsibility. However, the church's political responsibility begins with our being responsive to the God who has called us in baptism and wrenched a group of modern individuals away from the grip of the Empire. That makes us, well, peculiar. Even on Sunday morning.

I was visiting a congregation where, during the Sunday service, the preacher indulged in a practice not dear to my heart—a "children's sermon." The boys and girls were called down front. Squatting in the chancel, the preacher began: "Boys and girls, today is Epiphany. Can you say *Epiphany*? Epiphany falls on January 6, but today it falls on Sunday. Isn't that great, boys and girls? Epiphany means 'revelation,' 'manifestation.' A favorite Epiphany story is found at the beginning of Matthew's Gospel. You know the story. It's the story of the Wise Men who came to Bethlehem to see the baby Jesus. But they weren't really 'Wise Men' or even 'Three Kings.' The Bible calls them Magi. Magi. That's where we get our word *magic*. They were magicians, astrologers (the kind Mrs. Reagan uses). [No laughter in congregation.] They came 'from the East.' Some people think they came from Persia. Boys and girls, where is Persia? [Silence. One child ventures, "Iran?"]

"Yes. Iran. Good. That was Persia, but it wasn't all of Persia. What other countries are located in what was Persia?"

One child says, "Iraq?"

"Iraq! Good! Iraq. In fact, some people think these Magi came from Baghdad, capital of Iraq. There were lots of these Magi in Iraq. . . . And Matthew says these Magi, these Iraqis, *were the first to get an Epiphany, the first to see and to worship the baby Jesus*. A lot of people who had the Bible, a lot of people who thought they were close to God missed it and these strange people from Iraq saw it."

When the boys and girls were sent back to their parents in the pews, I noted that the congregation was fumbling for seatbelts. You tell a story like that, Sunday, 11:15 A.M., you don't know where we'll be headed by noon. The church has the oddest ways of going public, of being political. That sweet little children's sermon was preached on January 6, 1991, as the bombs were beginning to fall on Baghdad.

So go public with theology, if you dare. Just remember, it is peculiar, wonderfully, redemptively peculiar.

Reaching Out to the Gloom and Doomers

First there were the "Boomers," followed by the "Busters," to say nothing of "Yuppies," "Bumpies," and "Dinks." How we have labored to win them for the gospel, to attract them to the church! Now, according to a recently surfaced confidential memo by Stanley Greenberg, President Clinton's chief pollster, we must confront the rise of the people of "gloom and doom."

"Gloom and Doomers" are, says Greenberg, the "disillusioned working class and non-college" white electorate. Gloom and Doomers are "very negative" about the economy. Greenberg's national pool revealed them to be "dreadfully downscale" and decidedly for Dole. They have disproportionately no college degree, are women, and have incomes below the national average. Greenberg wonders how to reach these gloom-and-doom people for Clinton. I, of course, wonder how to get them into the church.

How can we make our churches inclusive, accessible, and user-friendly for the wallowers in gloom and doom? Having retooled ourselves, rearranged our music, shifted our sermons, and surrendered the Bible in behalf of the Boomers, Busters, and those who eat yogurt, I say it's time for us to cash in on the coming wave of gloom and doom.

The good news is that we may have relatively few adjustments to give the church a more positive image to those who are negative. Unlike our church-growth strategies with Yuppies and Dinks (Dual Income, No Kids), in which we had to suppress about two-thirds of Jesus' teaching—all of his unfortunate attacks upon the rich and the self-centered—Jesus is more congenial to the "felt needs" of the gloom-and-doom set.

Let's face it. Jesus despised politicians too. Unfortunately, he seems to have had as much contempt for conservatives as liberals, but we can use this. Jesus also believed the economy was going to hell in a handbasket, urging people to take their talents and wheel and deal while there was still time. Even though he ate often with tax collectors, this should not be taken as any sort of validation by the tax-and-spend policies of Democrats. Fortunately, Jesus not only thought the economy was going to hell in a handbasket, Jesus was negative about a number of other things as well—rich fools, rich young men, foolish virgins, mothers, mothers-in-law, older brothers, dogs. He even predicted the destruction of the Temple, and the moon in a weird hue.

How Norman Vincent Peale ever got Jesus to think positively, when you think about it, is a mystery. We must accentuate apocalyptic, eschatological texts. Face it, in the Bible there's a great deal more failure than success. Let the disciples in Mark's Gospel, the church at Laodicea, Pontius Pilate, and King Ahab be your model. The times are bad and always have been. Affluence has always been fragile. Let the parable of the thief at midnight be your favorite text, the "thief" being government regulation, the IRS, the ATF, the Department of Motor Vehicles, or whomever makes your Doomers the gloomiest. Chicken Little was right. The sky really is falling, and the megachurches of the future are those ready to cash in on the crash.

You say this approach does an injustice to the fullness of the gospel?

What about hope? What about "all things working together for good for those who are in Jesus Christ"?

Well, what about it? We have learned to jettison, to simplify, and to downsize the gospel in favor of the "felt needs" and the self-interests of so many, why not the children of gloom and doom? Rather than attack their predominant worldview, it is our job to adapt the church.

You say that you are pessimistic that this will work? You say that you expect that, though the gloom-and-doom generation is looking for something, it's not gospel. You say that you are negative about my proposal and that there are limits to how pliable we can make the church in the interest of meeting the needs of people who have not yet met Jesus?

Great! Pessimism and negativity are great market devices. We can work with that.

Hell, we can work with anything.

Campus Ministry *In Loco Parentis*

"The best campus ministers," she proclaimed, "tend to be older folk in their fifties, even sixties." Now why is that?

The *in loco parentis* approach to student life was in its death throes by the time I got to college as a student in the 1960s. By the time I returned to college as a chaplain in the 1980s, I could refer to this student generation not as those who had been overly parented, but rather as those who had been *abandoned* ("Reaching and Teaching the Abandoned Generation," *The Christian Century*, October 20, 1993, pp.187-90). They were on campus not with adults hovering over them *in loco parentis,* but rather they were wandering about with adults *in absentia.* Today's young adults have the dubious distinction of being our nation's most aborted generation. After scores of interviews with them, Susan Littwin called them "the postponed generation," those children of the children of the 1960s who were raised by parents so uncertain of their own values that they dared not attempt to pass on values to their young (*The Postponed Generation: Why America's Grown-Up Kids Are Growing Up Later,* Morrow and Co., 1986). *The Wall Street Journal* (July 28, 1993), in an article on the shrunken futures of today's recent college graduates, called them "the damned generation." Not too flattering a collection of labels for today's novice adults, but labels that may say more about our adult irresponsibility toward this generation than about problems with today's students.

I know of no better observer of this generation than one of its own, Vancouver novelist Douglas Coupland, a young writer whose novel *Generation X* (St. Martin's Press, 1991) provided one of the most popular ways of characterizing young adults today. In Coupland's most recent novel, *Life After God*, we see a series of snapshots of a generation wandering, the first generation, says Coupland, raised by parents who no longer even took the trouble not to believe in God.

I have never really felt like I was "from" anywhere; home to me ... is a shared electronic dream of cartoon memories, half-hour sitcoms, and national tragedies. I have always prided myself on my lack of accent—my lack of any discernible regional flavor. I used to think mine was a Pacific Northwest accent, from where I grew up, but then I realized my accent was simply the accent of nowhere—the accent of a person who has no fixed home in their mind. (*Life After God,* Pocket Books, 1994, p. 174)

Here is a generation, many of whom have never had enough sense of place, roots, or identity to consider themselves lost. "Lost" implies that one was once somewhere, that once there was a home. Speaking with some of his young adult friends, a character in *Life After God* exudes cynicism as he declares, "I know you guys think my life is some big joke—that it's going nowhere. But I'm happy. And it's not like I'm lost or anything. We're all too . . . middle class to ever be lost. Lost means you had faith or something to begin with, and the middle class never really had any of that. So we can never be lost. And you tell *me*, Scout—what is it we end up being, then—what exactly *is* it we end up being then—instead of being lost?" (p. 305).

Here is the way in which Chicago's Allan Bloom put the problem:

[T]he souls of young people are in a condition like that of the first men in the state of nature—spiritually unclad, unconnected, isolated, with no inherited or unconditional connection with anything or anyone. They can be anything they want to be, but they have no particular reason to want to be anything in particular. (*The Closing of the American Mind,* Simon and Schuster, 1987, p. 290)

I believe that communication of the gospel to this generation of young adults requires a rethinking of the task of our preaching. In speaking to "the abandoned generation," we are not calling them back to something they have previously known but have now forgotten; we are not attempting to open them up from a closed-minded provincialism of their childhood years; we are not doing cautious Christian nurture on youth who, having been raised in a basically Christian culture, now need a little spiritual nudge to cultivate the best that is within them. We are taking people to places they have never been, calling them to become part of a countercultural adventure called discipleship; assaulting them with a weird way of configuring the world called the gospel; adopting them, giving them a new home called church.

One of my congregations was next to a synagogue. The rabbi and I often had coffee on Mondays. Over coffee one Monday, I noted to the rabbi my surprise that our church was experiencing an influx of young adults, particularly single young adults of college age and just beyond. In my previous congregations this had been the most difficult age group to reach, thus my surprise to discover these young people returning to the church.

The rabbi replied, "Hardly a week goes by that we don't have some twenty-something person show up at the synagogue saying, 'I want to be a Jew again. My parents were only nominally Jewish, but I want to be Jewish for real.'"

"What is this?" I asked. "Is this part of the Reagan years, some new conservative trend?"

The rabbi said, "I think they're looking for their parents. We've got a generation who have been so inadequately parented that they are desperate for parents, roots, and identity. I think they're looking for their parents."

Church Growth

In one of my congregations, we decided that we needed to grow. We voted to launch a program of evangelism. Evangelism, you know what that means. It's the "We-had-better-go-out-and-get-new-members-or-we'll-die" syndrome. Beginning in the 1960s, our church had begun a two-decade decline in membership, so we figured that a little church-growth strategy was in order.

We studied a program from our denomination telling us how to get new members. Among other things, the church-growth program advocated a system of door-to-door visitation. So we organized ourselves into groups of two and, on an appointed Sunday afternoon, we set out to visit, to invite people to our church.

The teams went out, armed with packets of pamphlets describing our congregation, pamphlets telling about our denomination, fliers portraying me, the smiling pastor, inviting people to our church. Each team was given a map with the team's assigned street.

Helen and Gladys were given a map. They were clearly told to go down Summit Drive and to *turn right*. That's what they were told. I heard the team leader tell them, "You go down Summit Drive and turn right. Do you hear me, Helen? That's down Summit Drive and turn right?"

But Helen and Gladys, both approaching eighty, after lifetimes of teaching elementary school, were better at giving than receiving directions. They turned left, venturing down into the housing projects to the west of Summit Drive.

Which meant that Helen and Gladys proceeded to evangelize the wrong neighborhood and thereby ran the risk of evangelizing the wrong people.

Late that afternoon, each team returned to the church to make its report. Helen and Gladys had only one interested person to report to us, a woman named Verleen. Nobody on their spurious route was interested in visiting our church, nobody but Verleen. She lived with her two children in a three-room apartment in the projects, we were told. Although she had never been to a church in her life, Verleen wanted to visit ours.

This is what you get, I said to myself, when you don't follow directions, when you won't do what the pastor tells you to do; this is what you get, a woman from the projects named Verleen.

Next Sunday, Helen and Gladys proudly presented Verleen at the eleven o'clock service, Verleen along with two feral-looking children. Verleen liked the service so much, she said, that she wanted to attend the women's Thursday-morning Bible study. Helen and Gladys said they would pick her up.

On Thursday, Verleen appeared, proudly clutching her new Bible, a gift of Helen's circle, the first Bible Verleen had ever seen, much less owned.

I was leading the study that morning, a study on the lection for the coming Sunday: Luke 4, the story of Jesus' temptation in the wilderness. "Have any of you ever been faced with temptation and, with Jesus' help, resisted?" I asked the group after presenting my material. "Have any of you refused some temptation because of your Christian commitment?"

One of the women told about how, just the week before, there was some confusion in the supermarket checkout line and, before she knew it, she was standing in the supermarket parking lot with a loaf of bread that she had not paid for.

"At first I thought," she confessed, "Why should I pay for it? They have enough money here as it is. But then I thought, 'No, you are a Christian.' So I went back in the store and paid them for that loaf of bread."

I made some approving comment.

It was then that Verleen spoke. "A couple of years ago I was into cocaine really big. You know what that's like! You know how that stuff makes you crazy. Well, anyway, my boyfriend, not the one I've got now, the one who was the daddy of my first child, that one; well, we knocked over a gas station one night—got two hundred dollars out of it. It was as simple as taking candy from a baby. Well, my boyfriend, he says to me, 'Let's knock off that 7-Eleven down on the corner.' And something in me, it says, 'No, I've held up that gas station with you, but I ain't going to hold up no convenience store.' He beat the hell out of me, but I still said no. It felt great to say no, 'cause that's the only time in my life I ever said no to anything. Made me feel like I was somebody."

Through the stunned silence I managed to mutter, "Well, er, uh, that's resisting temptation. That's sort of what this text is about. And now it's time for our closing prayer."

After I stumbled out of the church parlor and was standing out in the parking lot helping Helen into her car, she said to me, "You know, I can't wait to get home and get on the phone and invite people to come next Thursday! Your Bible studies used to be dull. I think I can get a good crowd for this!"

I didn't know whether to laugh or cry. But the church, by the grace of God, grew.

WILLIAM H. WILLIMON

Baby Boomer Bloopers

I like Wade Clark Roof's *A Generation of Seekers: The Spiritual Journeys of the Baby Boom Generation* (Harper, 1993). I hope that he is right in his portrayal of spiritual restlessness among my generation. Note that I said, "*My* generation." One of my pet peeves in all this talk about "Baby Boomers" is the way a huge number of people have weaseled their way into *my* generation. How does Professor Roof get away with defining "Boomers" as those born between 1946 (the year of my nativity) and 1964 (the year of my high school graduation)? The difference in life experience between people who were born in 1946 and those who were born in 1964 is the difference between "The Ballad of Davy Crockett" and "I Can't Get No Satisfaction." By the way, Mick Jagger, of The Stones, and I were born the same year. What does that tell you?

The point of my peeve: No one ought to be called a Baby Boomer who wasn't conceived when the old man got off the boat from fighting the Big One (to my mind, the Korean Police Action and Vietnam don't count). *I* am a Baby Boomer. We're talking Ozzie and Harriet, Annette Funicello and the Mousketeers, Lassie, engagement rings, *The $64,000 Question,* and duck-and-cover exercises in the fifth grade here. If you can't sing the *Mickey Mouse Club* jingle by heart, if you didn't hear about the death of John Kennedy while you were in some high school cafeteria line, then you are not a Baby Boomer. I am a Boomer; you're not.

What was the name of the unseen philanthropist on "The Millionaire"? On the answer to that question rides membership in a generation.

Now, having established my credentials as an official Baby Boomer, I would like to have the last word on a few matters related to my generation. Wade Clark Roof (according to the Wofford College alumni directory) preceded me by enough years to be categorized as a pre-Boomer. Roof may be right in his contention that our generation are seekers, perpetual pilgrims in search of something else. Whether we are searching for the

Christian faith remains to be seen. I am deeply skeptical of our generation's ability to make the move from our essentially self-seeking and narcissistic posture to the faith of Jesus, but that is another sermon. I'm all for the church's understanding the spiritual aspirations of us Boomers and our heirs. Yet I also want us to confess that some of the church's failure to link up with this generation is due to the gap between the infatuations of this generation, and the stuff of the Christian faith.

Years ago I remember William Sloane Coffin (chaplain to the young of my generation) saying that one cannot easily make the move from the essential self-centeredness of our culture to the essential selflessness of Jesus. That move stands as a great obstacle for those who would positively plug in to the spiritual grope of the Boomers. A recent study of church growth and decline declares, "The evidence suggests that the boomer's relation to the church is fundamentally different from that of previous generations—that is, . . . consumer-oriented, captive to the subjective, expressive dimensions of cultural individualism" (David A. Roozen and C. Kirk Hadaway, *Church and Denominational Growth: What Does [or Does Not] Cause Growth or Decline*, Abingdon, 1993).

So, from one who ought to know, simply on the basis of having moved from "The Donna Reed Show" to "Cheers," here are what are for me the essential generational characteristics, the flotsam and jetsam of my generation:

1. We invented the sexual revolution. I am resentful when my students take on airs, acting as if they are the first generation in the history of the world to have discovered lust. We were the first generation of The Pill, "I Am Curious Yellow," and all that. Today's students are the result of our sexual revolution, not its cause.

Of course, we were also the first generation of divorce. In a sense, divorce as we have experienced it, was invented in the late 1960s. That makes today's young adults the children of the first generation of divorce, a fact that has great consequences for them.

2. We tend to float. Long-term, sustained attention upon any one issue is a problem for us. Burnout became our generation's accept-

able social disease. We learned that life involved work, sometimes sustained effort before there are results. Our much celebrated social activism in the 1960s wilted in the face of the tough facts of life. In 1967, *Time* called us "The Now Generation." When we can't have what we want (peace, justice, harmony) now, we become discouraged and distracted. The church, which tends to be here for the long haul, may have a problem keeping us focused.

3. We discovered dislocation. All of us remember where we were when we heard that John Kennedy had been shot. Many of us wandered forth from that event suspicious of the world, too dislocated to make much of an impact upon the world. Having put much faith in political antiheroes like Gene McCarthy and George McGovern, we then invented political cynicism. We withdrew into ourselves, into relentless scanning of, and untiring enhancement of, the self. Moving from "Don't trust anyone over thirty," we moved to "Don't trust any institution with over thirty members." How we will work out our anti-institutional bias in institutional religion remains to be seen.

Church, don't give up on us. Through the centuries, the poor old church has shown a rather amazing ability to say something and be something for each new generation. By the grace of God, it might also be there for us, Boomers that we are, moving us from life as *The Mary Tyler Moore Show,* or *Bonanza,* coaxing us toward the kingdom of God.

Operators Are Standing By

Just when I'm convinced that we really do live in the Secular City, I am struck by evidence that the demise of the deity is, as Mark Twain would say, greatly exaggerated. When I think of our elaborate intellectual defenses against the intrusion of God into our lives, I'm amazed that occasionally the Holy Spirit slips through our well-devised roadblocks, invades our tight, flat, myopic worldviews, and brings about revelation, even vocation.

On an otherwise secular Thursday morning one spring, I met

with a young man who complained that he was having difficulty sleeping at night. He was restless, found it difficult to study, even to go on a date. He was miserable. I told him that I had no competence in sleeping disorders and that if he wanted drugs he would have to see a psychiatrist.

"Why would you come here?" I asked. "I'm a pastor, not a psychologist." At that remark, he broke down in tears and said he thought God was trying to tell him something. He confessed he had often thought of going to seminary. Further conversation suggested to both of us that a vocation to the Christian ministry might indeed be part of his turmoil. I agreed to send him some material on various seminaries, and he agreed to talk with me again. "Try prayer rather than sleeping pills," I prescribed.

That very afternoon, a college senior had an appointment with me. Topic for discussion: Is it possible to be a pastor and still be a fully functioning human being? Translated: Are pastors ever allowed to have a "good time"?

We discussed the specifics of her idea of a good time. I told her she could not be a pastor unless she was as dignified, serious, pious, and sober as I. She failed to take me seriously. We then explored her growing sense of Christian vocation and some options for seminary, and I described some of the fun-loving preachers I had known.

By this time I was ready to tell people whom God was calling to take a number and get in line.

That evening I ate at a very fancy restaurant, one of those places with apricot carpeting, apricot napkins, apricot tablecloths. As part of a medical school search committee, I was joining other members in taking a candidate to dinner. Early in the evening, our waiter asked me, "Aren't you a clergyman?" I was embarrassed, and the medical school staff made a few wisecracks.

"How did you know?" I asked the watier. "Perhaps you have seen our service on television."

"No," he replied. "You just look like you would probably be a minister."

Many more wisecracks followed from the pill-pushers. "What could I do to get away from the waiter?" I wondered.

We finally finished the meal, talked a while, then left. On our way out the door, the waiter came running after me, calling, "Wait, Reverend!"

Oh no, I thought, he expects a larger tip.

"Reverend, which seminary do you think is best for a Baptist who feels called to the ministry?"

The next morning I led a group Bible study on the book of Acts of the Apostles. In the middle of our study, someone exclaimed, "Angels, angels! What are we supposed to do with all these angels that Acts talks about? I've never seen or talked to an angel, nor has anyone I've ever known."

I told her about my experience the day before. "Just be patient," I said. "Take a number. Wait your turn. The angels are busy just now—taking messages to Duke University sophomores, banging on their brains all night long; harassing collegiate hell-raisers, calling waiters in fancy French restaurants. Give them time. Take a number. They'll get to you as soon as they can."

Secularity Lite

I always said the only ministry that I never wanted any part of was the institutional kind. While I considered it fine for others to be chaplains at colleges, hospitals, or airports, I knew it was definitely not for me.

A chaplain friend at a state college confirmed my feeling. The one subject perennially popular among college students is sex, right? Wrong. He once spent two years planning a regional symposium on sex and Christian values. He invited a number of controversial and nationally recognized experts on sex. Three people showed up the first night of the series. That was three more than showed up the second night, so he cancelled the rest of the series. Perhaps it was the religious aspect that scared students away.

And yet here I am at Duke University, functioning as an institutional chaplain. God is funny that way. Don't ever let God hear you say out loud what you are not going to do. When I began this job, I knew I would continue to enjoy familiar pastoral acts—

counseling, preaching, teaching, praying, and leading Bible studies. However, I wanted strictly to avoid being the university's
public relations person. I didn't want to lead prayers before football games or in basketball locker rooms or at the groundbreaking
of the new engineering building.

"You are now in a thoroughly secular setting," I told myself.
"You are in an institution that does not support the church's goals
or values. In other words, you will have to work very hard to keep
your categories neat and clean. Do not be disappointed when people look upon you as a cog within the vast academic machinery
rather than as a pastor and a person of God."

But on the job I have found the sacred often getting all mixed
up with the secular. One term I went reluctantly—out of a sense
of duty—to the semester's final faculty meeting, which preceded
a social hour. I thought it would be good for the university minister to be seen in public, mixing with the faculty, so people would
not forget me. "I will just run over, get a bit to eat, smile and go
home," I told myself. "I will simply make an appearance.
Everyone there will be academic and secular, moving in a direction other than the one I represent."

"Aren't you the minister?" someone asked me shortly after I
arrived. "I have been wondering if you have thought about how
the theory of relativity relates to traditional Christian concepts of
prayer." He was a distinguished professor of physics. I was a
Methodist minister who had not the slightest idea what he was
talking about.

I eased my way over to the chips and dip. As I reached toward
the table, a woman said, "A student and I were discussing your
sermon from a couple of weeks ago. Would you send me a copy?"

I told her I was flattered and would be delighted to do so.
"What was it that you liked about my sermon?" I asked.

"I didn't say we liked it. We were studying the difference
between the way the brain works in regard to religious thought as
opposed to scientific thought, and I figured your sermon would
serve as an interesting case study," she said.

I wanted to remind her that I was simply there to make an
appearance, have a bit to eat and something to drink, and go

home. I was off duty. My meter was not running. I was in a secular environment. She and her colleagues were not interested in the things I do.

As I was trying to make my way out the door, an older professor of geology approached me and asked, "Have you done any work on glossolalia? My wife and I have become very interested in this subject. Could you recommend a good book on it?"

I scurried down the steps and out to my car. It is such a drag to be God's representative in such a secular environment.

Open the Door

Acts 2 does the birthday of the church, the gift of the Spirit, in rock music and Technicolor. In jubilant, triumphant wind and fire, the church is born.

Most of my congregations fit John's honest description of Pentecost—a confused, dispirited group huddled behind locked doors on Easter evening (John 20:19-23).

Oh sure, the women had said, "We have seen the Lord," but we did not believe them. We said, "Women sometimes become emotional, hysterical, particularly in time of grief." And there has been much grief this first Easter weekend. That's what death, unrelenting, uninterrupted death and defeat does to people.

Thus I, as a pastor, have often been surprised by Paul's claim that, "When I was among you I decided to know nothing except Jesus Christ and him crucified," as if the church's big problem was an overdose of Easter, unbridled enthusiasm, too much resurrection.

I've not served that church.

Most of my congregations have known nothing but crucifixion, death, or at least slow, unmitigated congregational decay. Empty Sunday school rooms, faded church school literature stacked in the corner, a copy of *Together* magazine with a cover picture of the president shaking hands with a Methodist bishop. I don't recognize the bishop, but the president is Eisenhower.

Unlike Paul, I say, "Alas, you were so dead, that when I was among you I tried to preach nothing but Jesus Christ and him resurrected."

I did not preach that, for if the church failed to believe Mary, breathless back from the tomb, why should it believe me? In matters ecclesial, congregational, death is omnivorous, and gospel becomes the "good news" that last year The United Methodists only lost about fifty-five thousand members—a few thousand less than the year before. When news like that is *good*, don't expect people to believe Mary about Easter.

So the church gathered on Easter night to mourn, to retreat, to huddle behind our locked doors for fear. John says our lock-in was "for fear of the Jews." That is an image for anyone, any people, any event, we do not understand, cannot contain or control—like Easter.

Then suddenly, Jesus stood among them and greeted them with "Peace be with you." He showed them the holes in his hands and side. He breathed upon them an empowering breath of the Holy Spirit, the same breath with which he blew open their locked door. "Receive the Holy Spirit," he said.

In Acts 2, Luke says the Holy Wind nearly knocked the doors off the hinges. In John 20, the Holy Wind was no more than a breath, but it was enough to blow open a securely locked door. Pentecost is an Easter evening draft through a locked door. On Pentecost 'John 20' our lock-in became a break-in.

Do you believe it?

A pastor told me about how his congregation built a new building on a plot of ground willed to them by a parishioner. Trouble was, the lot was perilously close to a "bad section" of town.

"People warned us," said the pastor, "that we were building in the wrong neighborhood."

But build there they did and, as predicted, scarcely a week after the church was opened, there was a break-in. The front door had been pushed open. Someone had entered the church. "You could see the footprints, but we couldn't find anything missing." They looked in the office, the pastor's study, the sacristy. Everything was in its place.

They put new, better, locks on the doors.

Two weeks later, the janitor found one of the windows in the women's restroom had been forced open. Again, there were a few muddy footprints; again, nothing was missing.

They put new, better, locks on the windows.

A few days later, to their dismay, someone left one of the doors unlocked; and again, footprints were evidence of entry, and again, nothing had been taken.

"Then one day the janitor said, 'This is a strange church. I worked for the Baptists downtown, and they never used much toilet paper. But you Episcopalians have used two big boxes in your first month.'"

The pastor realized what the intruders had been stealing. "I fell to my knees," he said, "tears in my eyes, murmuring, 'God help us to be your church. With such great need around us, we don't have to be much of a church to do your will.'"

Some said, despite locked doors, they felt a breeze.

A Big Church

It was a big church—large, downtown, Episcopal. Get the picture? It wasn't what one would call a "megachurch" (I told you, it was an *Episcopal* church), but it was a big church, bigger even than numbers can tell.

I had been speaking there for their noonday Lenten series. I had just preached, rather eloquently I might add, on Ephesians 3:18-19 where the writer prays "that you may have the power to comprehend, with all the saints, what is the breadth and length and height and depth, and to know the love of Christ that surpasses knowledge, so that you may be filled with all the fullness of God."

My sermon was short (I told you, it was an *Episcopal* church), but it had a big biblical thought behind it. I told them that Ephesians 3:18-19 is a little prayer asking for big things for the church.

At the lunch after the service (the lunch prepared and served by volunteers in the church fellowship hall), our table was served by a young man who wore a nametag saying, "David—Integrity." I immediately recognized him as a member of Integrity, the Episcopal group of gay Christians. The rector spoke jovially with David as David served us. I was introduced to David. David volunteered that the congregation "has been an answer to my prayer."

"I *love* this church and these people!" he exclaimed.

"David gets thirty dollars an hour to wait tables in the best restaurant in town," bragged the rector, "but we get him for free here at these lunches because he loves us so much."

Making conversation with the rector during the meal, I asked him about Integrity and its relationship to their congregation. "Did you get any resistance to their meeting here?" I asked. I told you that it was a big, downtown, Episcopal church.

"Resistance?" the rector responded. "I suppose so, but that's part of the job, isn't it? After all, they weren't *my* idea, they're not *my* group."

I asked him what he meant by that.

"I mean by that just what I meant when one of our members came to me to complain about 'Why you want to have *those people* come to our church.' I asked him, '*I* want to have them? What on earth do you mean by that? Their presence here is not *my* idea. *I* didn't invite them. Why on earth would *I* want them? Let the record show that *I* didn't invite *you* either. Why on earth would *I* have invited *you*? Let's get this straight once and for all,' I told him, 'This is *God's* church, not mine, certainly not yours. This is *God's* idea of a good time, *God's* idea of a fun bunch of people, not mine.'"

There you have it. The church is God's idea of a good time, God's idea of a fun bunch of people.

One of the great weaknesses of our current stress upon the importance of pastoral personality, the need for pastors to be open and loving and accepting, is that we get confused into believing that the pastor somehow sets the boundaries for and determines the "breadth and length and height and depth" of the graciousness of God in the church. No. The church is the gathering of God. When church growth or evangelism means the search for "people like us," the saints are denied the "power to comprehend" just how effusive, extravagant God means to be with God's grace.

One of the most challenging, as well as most invigorating, tasks of the saints is the constant struggle in our little minds "to comprehend . . . what is the breadth and length and height and depth" of the love of Christ, that love which clearly surpasses our knowledge. It's big.

The next day, visiting with troubled members of another denomination, Southern Baptists, a denomination in great pain over just who is in the church and just who isn't, one of the pastors said something that made me think of that brash rector at the big church.

"Do you know what is for me the most comforting passage in all of Scripture right now?" he asked. "It is there in the Gospel of John where Jesus says, 'I am going to prepare a place for you . . . because in my Father's house are many rooms.'"

"Comforting?" I asked.

"Comforting," he responded. "We usually read that passage from John at funerals. But it ought to be read as a comforting word at major church meetings. Too many people in my denomination want a smaller church with fewer rooms. They want a room just big enough to hold them and their close friends in the faith. But Jesus has promised that his Father's house is a great, big house, one with lots and lots of rooms. That's a great comfort in a time when there are many who want to scale down the church."

I've been in lots of churches. I've never been in one that was large enough fully to embody the expansive grace of God. Maybe that's why we need lots of churches, churches with lots and lots of rooms. We need churches always willing to add on another wing to the Father's house.

Maybe that's why the best thing we could do for our people as pastors is to constantly pray "that you may have the power to comprehend, with all the saints, what is the breadth and length and height and depth, and to know the love of Christ that surpasses knowledge, so that you may be filled with all the fullness of God."

The Body of Christ

The day I met John he was still a bit shaken from his participation in the previous Sunday's Eucharist. John directs a Kairos Prison Ministry in Florida. One Sunday his team was leading worship in the gymnasium of a Florida maximum security prison. Without warning, one of the prisoners sprang to his feet, attacked a fellow inmate and, in John's words, "disemboweled him right there." An Episcopal layperson on John's team, a physician, aided the injured man for over an hour, but the man died.

Kairos goes into some of our nation's worst prisons, attempting to form Christian communities. Beginning on Friday evening, a Kairos team meets with willing prisoners for an intense weekend retreat. After the weekend, Kairos offers continuing, regular support for the new Christian community through monthly return trips to the prison, correspondence, and counsel.

The prisoners badly need this support. "It's a bit frightening to know that a person who converts to Christ during one of our retreats will probably be assaulted by other prisoners during the week. A fierce, unyielding conformity is enforced within the prison. It doesn't pay for a prisoner to go back to his cell and say, 'Hey, I'm a Christian.' We have returned, a week after a retreat, to find that one of our recent converts has been beaten to death because of his baptism."

While Kairos is ecumenical, it puts great stress upon the sacramental nature of the Christian community. "A major aspect of our work," says John, "is giving chocolate chip cookies."

"Churchpeople on the outside bake the cookies, the real good kind with lots of chips and nuts. We take these cookies in with us and give each person on retreat a bag to take back to the cell. Some of the prisoners may never have received a gift in their whole lives. And we tell them, 'You're Christians now. Jesus told us to bless those who persecute us. You can use these cookies in his name. Offer them to anyone who tries to beat you up.'

"Most of these people are so full of hate and anger that we put a lot of stress on forgiveness," John says. "A good way for inmates to know that Jesus forgives them is to forgive someone else. So we ask them to find the person they hate the most, offer that person a cookie and say, 'I'm going to love you, and give my hate up for good.'

"Invariably, a new Christian will then be well on the way to making another. 'Man, I don't know what you've got, but I want it,' other inmates say."

In the U.S., 30 to 70 percent of those released from prison go back. But a recent Colorado study of men and women who had experienced Kairos's ministry showed that fewer than 10 percent returned.

And he took a chocolate chip cookie, and broke it, saying, Take, eat; this is my body, which is given for you; this do in remembrance of me.

The Unassimilatable Mr. Gomes

Peter Gomes, ninth Plummer professor of Christian morals, and minister of Memorial Church at Harvard University, is for me a model of how ministry to a university ought to be done. While too many other once-great university chapels are empty, Gomes eloquently preaches to an appreciative full house.

What makes Gomes successful?

The answer in great part has to do with his dogged determination to articulate the Christian faith in an environment that knows many things except Jesus. The soul of Christian ministry on all too many campuses has been reduced to an amorphous blob called "the ministry of presence." Go stand next to whatever crowd may form and call that "ministry." Gomes prefers to characterize his work at Memorial Church as prophetic "embarrassment and rebuke." In the middle of Harvard Yard, Memorial Church is somewhat of an embarrassment to the secularity that currently holds captive most universities. One year, Harvard University's president, Derek Bok, stirred national interest with his call for the restoration of "ethics." The evangelical Puritans who founded Harvard could have told Bok what he does not yet know: There's no such thing as "ethics" floating around out there. There is only ethics as an expression of a worldview, an account of reality, a particular story about what is true. There are only "Christian" ethics, "pagan" ethics, "utilitarian" ethics.

Gomes is also a rebuke to a pluralism that acts as if truth were a matter of personal opinion. Against some vague notion of "presence," Gomes prefers to characterize his work at Harvard as mission. "This place is a wonderful mission field, a world populated by those who have not had the opportunity to take seriously the gospel. My audience is very cultured, very sophisticated, very uninformed about the gospel."

Under Gomes's fifteen years of leadership, Memorial Church has reacted to the secular majority not by reducing the church's message to the lowest common denominator, but rather by stressing the peculiarities and particularities of this faith. Gomes's chief strength, when compared to many others who flounder in campus ministry, is that he knows who he is, by whom he is called, and to whom he is ultimately accountable. His ministry is joyfully, unambiguously Protestant Christian.

Peter Gomes loves to tell the story of the time he was visiting with some random dean of Harvard. The dean beckoned Gomes over to his window, inviting him to admire the wonderful view of Memorial Church from the dean's office.

"You know," said the dean, "I'm sure if we were doing this again, we would never put Memorial Church in so prominent a location, right in the middle of Harvard Yard."

Gomes, never one to float past bait offered by a pompous pagan, replied, "Well, we're there. And we're not moving. Get used to it."

One undergraduate explained that she attended Memorial Church rather than a service elsewhere because, "I don't need to get up at 11 A.M. to hear a homiletical rehash of the Op-Ed page of the *New York Times*. Gomes actually has something new and interesting to say."

The basic gospel has become so rare that it's again become interesting.

Rather than escape into the socially approved activities of

providing psychological counseling for the students, trying to out-secular the secularists, out-assimilate the assimilationists, and giving away the store in the process, Gomes points proudly to the services and ministry of Memorial Church as an "unassimilatable lump" in the middle of dear old Harvard.

"God must have a sense of humor," says Gomes, "to keep a visible Christian community here in order to keep the university anxious and nervous."

It's time for more of us clergy beyond the bounds of Harvard Yard to be anxious and nervous about who we are and what we're doing.